Twilight Time

Twilight Time
Aging in Amazement

SUSIE KAUFMAN

RESOURCE *Publications* · Eugene, Oregon

TWILIGHT TIME
Aging in Amazement

Copyright © 2019 Susie Kaufman. All rights reserved. Except for brief quotations in critical publications or reviews, no part of this book may be reproduced in any manner without prior written permission from the publisher. Write: Permissions, Wipf and Stock Publishers, 199 W. 8th Ave., Suite 3, Eugene, OR 97401.

Resource Publications
An Imprint of Wipf and Stock Publishers
199 W. 8th Ave., Suite 3
Eugene, OR 97401

www.wipfandstock.com

PAPERBACK ISBN: 978-1-5326-8085-4
HARDCOVER ISBN: 978-1-5326-8086-1
EBOOK ISBN: 978-1-5326-8087-8

Manufactured in the U.S.A.   APRIL 12, 2019

For my sister, Roberta Maisel

She opened my eyes and paved the way.

Ten thousand flowers in spring, the moon in autumn,
a cool breeze in summer, snow in winter.
If your mind isn't clouded by unnecessary things,
this is the best season of your life.

—Wu-men, thirteenth century

Contents

Permissions | ix
Preface | xi
Acknowledgments | xiii

No Time like the Present | 1
Rebbe Nachman in Costa Rica | 3
Invoking the Ancestors | 6
Black and White | 9
Living Arrangements | 11
Paleolithic Father's Day | 13
Going Home | 16
Acceleration | 19
Tragedy in the Tropics | 22
In Tobago | 24
Coming and Going | 27
Roll Over Beethoven | 30
Witness | 32
Americana | 35
Not Yet | 38
A Pebble of Regret | 41
The Sunny Side of the Street | 43
Shattered Glass | 46
On Children | 49

Minnesota August | 51
The Empathy Strikes Back | 54
On Drowning | 57
Talk to Me | 59
They Can't Take That Away from Me | 61
Trade-In | 64
Sintra Socks | 67
Coco Loco | 70
What Slips through Your Fingers | 72
The Persistence of Nature | 74
Less Time, More Space | 76
Beyond Nostalgia | 79
Improv in the Subjunctive | 82
On Another Note | 84
Just in Case | 87
End of Day | 89

Permissions

"Ten thousand flowers in spring, the moon in autumn" (Wu-Men) from THE ENLIGHTENED HEART: AN ANTHOLOGY OF SACRED POETRY, EDITED by STEPHEN MITCHELL. Copyright © 1989 by Stephen Mitchell. Reprinted by permission of HarperCollins Publishers.

"Bewitched, Bothered and Bewildered" (from *Pal Joey*) Words by LORENZ HART Music by RICHARD RODGERS © 1941 (renewed) WB MUSIC CORP. and WILLIAMSON MUSIC CO. All rights reserved. Used by permission of ALFRED MUSIC.

"Bewitched" by Richard Rodgers and Lorenz Hart © 1941 Chappell & Co. Inc. Copyright renewed and assigned to Williamson Music (for the extended renewal period) and Wb Music Corp. for the USA. International copyright secured. All rights reserved. Used by permission.

"The abyss yawns but it does not sleep," text attached to drawing by Linda Baker-Cimini, © 2011 Used by permission.

Henry A. Giroux, "Normalizing Trump's Authoritarianism Is Not an Option," *Tikkun* (January 19, 2017) Used by permission.

Preface

FROM an early age, I have wondered about mortality, about birth and death, and all the pigeons and sweet rolls in between. It remains amazing to me that life begins and ends with such majesty, rocketing in and out of consciousness, but leaves behind it a field littered with small details, the oneness of things fragmented into kaleidoscopic diversity. In my fifties and sixties, I worked for some years as a hospice chaplain. I had no particular credentials, only a fascination with people's stories. I was not Catholic like most of the patients, so I could not approach the bedside with particular prayers and rituals. Instead, I listened for meaning. I listened for the melody of people's lives as they met up with impermanence.

This book is entitled *Twilight Time* because it is in the waning light of my life that I have come to embrace evanescence. My days are nothing more than the life span of a firefly writ large. But while I'm here, I am *aging in amazement*. I am awed by what I have seen and what I continue to see. Much of the past is blurry. Still, some memories leap out and take me by surprise, like a child jumping out from behind a tree in a game of hide-and-seek. The clownish blue eye shadow my mother applied with such enthusiasm. The stunning grilled eggplant I ate in the Piazza di Santa Croce in Florence. The famished, unintelligible drone of my uncle rushing headlong through the Haggadah at Passover. At seventy-three, I am swimming in the stuff of my life, doing what I do. I am making meaning.

Preface

In this collection of short essays, I see myself wandering in the wilderness of my own late-in-life thinking and feeling. I meander. The reflections are not arranged chronologically or thematically. They bounce off one another by some associative magic, as if I am stretched out on the chaise on my back porch, allowing the memories and images to come and go before I descend into an afternoon nap. They are partial, sometimes dreamlike. For the most part, these essays appeared originally on my blog *seventysomething* (susiekaufman.blogspot.com) or were read at IWOW (In Words Out Words), a monthly open mic in the Berkshires, where I have been blessed to live for the past forty-six years.

We all share the basic outlines of this story of arrival and departure, but each of us is wondrously particular. I offer here a glimpse of the consciousness of an older woman, specifically a woman raised in a secular Jewish household in mid-century New York, now looking back at the texture of her inhabited past and the empty expanse of her unknowable future. As I have written in one of the last essays in this collection, "Not-knowing is the final frontier." I live every day in the awareness that I have no idea how much longer I'll be here on this planet. I don't know the shape and duration of my dying. I don't know if I will predecease my husband or if he will leave me to figure it all out on my own. All I know is I once spoke at length in pidgin Spanish on the subject of Jewish mysticism with an Argentine woman on a bus in Costa Rica. This must be enough. There is a cast-iron pot on the back burner of my brain where all my experiences are simmering. The stew is bubbling and flavorful. In gratitude, I offer you a taste.

Acknowledgments

I am grateful to Matthew Wimer and the staff at Wipf and Stock for shepherding this book into print. Their expertise and graciousness have been a support at every step along the way.

My dear friend Jinks Hoffman believed in me and encouraged me to embark on this project when my own faith wavered.

I am fortunate to have a friend of more than fifty years who is a professional copy editor. Judi Kales read the manuscript of this book word by word, comma by comma. Her gentle guidance has been invaluable.

Aïda Garcia Pons helped me with matters technological. Her kindness lifted my spirits.

Along with many other writers, poets, and musicians, I am grateful to Deb Koffman for providing the space for us to share our work at her monthly open mic, IWOW (In Words Out Words). IWOW has been a house of worship for me over the years.

It has been an inspiration to share the stage on a number of occasions with Joan Embree, a courageous and gifted writer.

Some twenty years ago, Virginia Finn opened my heart to spirit. Life became much larger after Virginia.

I have been blessed by many years of reading and talking about books with my son, Isaac Kaufman. To love someone who loves books is a great thing.

My remarkable husband, Frank Gioia, has taught me more about life and art than I thought there was to know. From Frank I have discovered that the learning never ends.

No Time like the Present

LET me tell you about seventy. It's a time approaching the outer reaches of the imagination, nesting between your hardworking middle years and the coming unraveling of old age. You are visited by a gathering party of imperfections, eyesight dimming, conversation punctuated by the what? what? of hearing loss. You wake up with a stiffness in the thoracic spine, a dicey corner where the backbone meets the neck. To get past this stiffness, you are required to do a series of stretches, one that you're partial to because it makes you feel like a Balinese dancer, which you most assuredly are not. Nouns, especially proper nouns, have deserted the sinking ship of your brain. In your more philosophical moments, you explore the deep meaning of this, the way the mind retains verbs, the act of weeding the garden, but does not always recognize the word trowel. Verbs seem to be primal: how you move, what you do, a window into your animal nature. Nouns are the window dressing that you can do without, or google.

In your writing, you dive headlong into the murky swamp of your past, dragging it kicking and screaming into the unsuspecting present. You visit versions of your Upper West Side Jewish family; the airless narrow passageways you navigated growing up in the well-dressed sliver between Central Park and Riverside Drive, the biggest small town in America. You watch wide-eyed as tsunamis of sixties sexual exploration, political upheaval, and spiritual searching wash up on the shore. You make a life for yourself using the materials at hand: your well-intentioned shopkeeper parents;

your sister, a half generation older; a Boston-Irish spiritual director who urges you to invite God to lunch; and your Italian-American husband, whose very being demonstrates daily that a great world exists outside of your own limited experience.

You had to arrive at seventy to articulate these themes, to reach out and touch Otherness, to see the One in the Many. Despite forgetting the names of people you meet on the street in Stockbridge, you seem to have an enhanced memory of the sense of things from the past. You can feel the claustrophobic space of a self-service elevator where a teenage boy assaults you as a little girl. You can smell the stale air of the Amtrak train where you first meet your husband on your way home from visiting your father in the hospital. You can explore your inner vision, even as your capacity to read small print is fading.

The line between life and art is becoming indistinct as well. Here you are in the full bloom of grandmahood, sending out your collection of essays. The familiar cloud of uncertainty, the sense that your life was dripping down the drain, that you had failed to make something of yourself, has suddenly cleared. It occurs to you that you always wanted to be an investigative reporter. You always wanted to dig and dig, interpret and interpret. And now, here you are at seventysomething enjoying the opportunity to make meaning out of your own life, an antidote to the mayhem all around you. But you cannot make meaning if you keep the past tied up in ribbons of nostalgia. You have to unwrap it, examine it, play with it, shape it, and give it language. You have to make art. You could not have done this when you were younger. You did not have the courage. Now, it seems, there is nothing to lose and only awareness to gain.

Rebbe Nachman in Costa Rica

As far as I know, Nachman of Bratslav did not winter in Costa Rica. The late-eighteenth-century Hasidic rebbe remained tucked away in Ukraine, warmed by the fires of fervent prayer while the snow piled high on his doorstep. Still, walking on the beach, I thought of his famous words, "All the world's a very narrow bridge . . . The essential thing is not to fear at all." With this in mind, I abandoned all previous identities. I let go of bookworm, acrophobic, fried couch potato, and signed up for a rain-forest excursion that featured crossing a series of canopy bridges leading to a waterfall. It was Juan the guide, a young couple from California, and me. I cast myself in the role of the determined older woman who deserved no end of credit for her courage. The hike began with a climb of more than an hour up rough-hewn stone steps interspersed with other steps made out of discarded motorcycle tires filled with dried mud. The journey had the quality of a pilgrimage, something along the lines of Our Lady of Fátima, only upright, without the part where the devotees walk on their knees. The ascent in the sultry jungle heat was definitely a test. It seemed to be designed to wear me down, so that by the time we arrived at the canopy bridges, my resistance was exhausted. There was no turning back.

It's not often that you encounter a spiritual exercise made literally manifest. All the world really is a narrow bridge! I had planned to say the Sh'ma each time I crossed over. This prayer, central to Jewish practice, proclaims the Divine Oneness of all things. It is said every day by observant Jews, but also at the moment of death, to indicate that the essence of the person is about to return to its source, to the All. I imagined that it would balance out the narrow-bridge effect, fortifying me with a connection to the sky, the vegetation, the birds—reconfiguring the landscape so the fear couldn't get me. I thought about saying the Sh'ma when I stepped out onto the first span, but I made the mistake of not waiting until Juan got to the other side. The bridge rocked up and down and swung back and forth like a pendulum under his footfall. After that, I forgot about praying and just waited my turn. Everything was still. All I had to do was put one foot in front of the other.

After crossing ten or twelve rope bridges and descending the slope on more improvised steps, we arrived at the promised waterfall. I had already been swimming in the high-saline Pacific for many days, as well as in a chlorinated pool in an area that featured a faint septic smell. Nothing could prepare me for the clarity of the cascading rain-forest water, clean like the unmediated joy of a baby's smile. It seemed to be absolutely transparent, with no solid precipitates. It was invitingly cold and regenerating, just the right ritual of purification after the sweaty trials of the day.

Safely back in Manuel Antonio, massaging my feet and considering the spiritual integration of climbing, crossing, and immersion, I thought of another of Rebbe Nachman's aphorisms. If you believe breaking is possible, believe fixing is possible. It was noon, and I hadn't thought about Betsy DeVos since early in the morning. When the shadow of her malignant presence reappeared in my awareness, I realized that in our current situation, it is no exercise of the imagination to believe that breaking is possible. Everywhere we see the intentional dismantling, the fracturing, of democratic norms and institutions we naively thought were inviolable.

It's a stretch in this environment to believe that fixing is possible. In order to get to that place, we will have to exercise our capacity for vision. There will be a long climb over rocky and unfamiliar territory. We may be called upon to put one foot in front of the other and step out onto a narrow bridge that doesn't feel entirely safe, and then another bridge, and another. Like the mystery of childbirth, getting from breaking to fixing will require faith, endurance, and hard labor. We will have to stick together, hold on to the redemptive image of the waterfall, and wear good shoes. The essential thing is not to fear.

Invoking the Ancestors

My guests and I invited our grandparents to the Seder, and they came, in steerage, carrying bundles. My great-grandmother hides her silver candlesticks in her skirts during the long journey from Romania. Now they sit at the Seder table. Our grandparents came from Budapest and Moldova. They came from Santa Margherita di Belice in western Sicily and from Minsk. From Limerick and Calabria and from Lodz, though the last could not be remembered as they were in life. Only their names could be offered, a spectral afterimage of the people they were before they perished in the Shoah. Still, they were with us. They were all with us. Our minyan of ten, a few still in their sixties but the rest seventysomethings, crowded together at the table, sharing the Haggadot, reaching over one another to get to the charoset. Remarkably, there was still more than enough room for our ancestral guests.

Both of my grandfathers died before I was born. One, the patriarch of a large family, flourished into the Depression as the proprietor of a dry goods store on First Avenue. The other, Grandpa Louis, died all the way back in 1923. I inherited from my mother an ice-cold antipathy for him, a man I never met. In the only photograph of him that remains, my mother works at being playful for the camera, sticking her head out between her parents. He is dapper in white shoes. You would never know that she always used the words *stern* and *austere* when describing him. But who can say? He might have been affectionate if he'd known me. He might have been the kind of grandfather who came to visit with candy bars and jump ropes in his jacket pocket, the kind of grandfather who would stroke your hair and kiss your forehead. Instead, he's a cipher who left behind nothing but a sour dread. Seders on my mother's side were led by my uncle, who mumble-davened for hours on end, not seeming to care whether anyone else understood the exodus from Egypt, the matzoh and maror.

My Hungarian paternal grandmother died when I was five and left me with only two memories, both pungent. In the first, she answers the door of the railroad flat on 107th Street, a dense thicket of antimacassars and porcelain figurines. We ring the bell, the door swings open. There she is with her arms spread wide, ready to engulf us, shrieking "Who's who in America?" No austerity on that side of the family. Everything about them was deafening and supersized. In the second memory, she's sitting on the terrible, scratchy, needlepoint sofa in our living room. I'm on her lap. It's a good thing, because it protects my little-girl legs from the aggressively abrasive upholstery. After a while, I start to suffocate in the surround of her enormous breasts. Sitting on the sofa unprotected would be better than having my face pressed into her perfumed cleavage. Seders on my father's side dispensed with the praying altogether in short order and went on to loud and insistent demands for soup.

All but one of the grandparents we invited, along with Elijah, to drink too much and eat copious amounts of food were born in Europe. They crossed the Atlantic reading Yiddish newspapers, speaking in Sicilian dialect. They were small businessmen, glorified peddlers. They were tailors and plasterers. They lived in tenements and brownstones, inhaled garlicky air and drank homemade wine and bathtub gin. My Romanian grandmother, Anna, the only one of that generation I really knew, used to like to tell me about pogroms in Jassy when she was a girl. How Cossacks tossed rocks through the windows of the Jewish households. How in 1892, hundreds of Jewish shops were closed down, tradesmen driven out of the city. The following year, Anna and her family made Pesach in New York.

The essential story—the fleeing, the pursuit, the crossing, the wilderness, the illusion of arrival—goes on and on, up to this moment. Everything is and has always been provisional. Roots are for trees. Our origins are fluid, our stories oceanic and subject to changing tides of interpretation, the interventions of history. They say my grandfather Louis became unhinged in something called the Panic of 1907 when he lost what little money he had. The financial upset in the year of my mother's birth and its attendant sense of failure and foreboding impacted the entire family saga. It's an elusive, but mesmerizing narrative, one of the many fragments floating over the Seder table when we gathered our ancestors around us this Pesach.

Black and White

THERE were two alternate realities. One was the Wedgwood sky, the peeled-bark sycamores, the amethyst ring that your mother wore, and the sealskin coat that you buried your face in when she put it on in winter. All over the world, there was color and dimensionality, even if some people were seeing the vast Saharan sands and some people were seeing the red and green of the traffic lights flashing on and off. You walked into that reality and you touched it. You walked through the front door of the apartment off Broadway, down the blue carpeted hallway, and you gave your father a peck on the cheek, scratching your face on the bristles of his mustache. You kept going, past the mahogany dining room table where he ate his broiled lamb chops, the curio cabinet filled with his pillbox collection, tiny bonbons of silver and enamel. Past the bathroom, all porcelain with octagonal tiles, and the bedrooms, yours with spectacularly ugly maple furniture. This was one reality for you. Even now, it is more deeply imprinted than anything you've encountered in the decades since.

But there was another reality. This appeared on the small screen of the clunky living-room Zenith and, on Saturday mornings, on the larger screen in the popcorn-infused Loew's Eighty-third Street, where the power-crazed matrons with flashlights harassed you. This reality was all black and white. Sid Caesar speaking phony foreign languages, Dinah Shore advertising Chevrolet, Fred Astaire soft-shoeing. All black and white. And newsreels of presidents without orange hair and disasters where the blood was charcoal gray. This version of the world, two-tone and two-dimensional, felt so real at the time that when you saw Bobby Kennedy speaking to a crowd on Amsterdam Avenue, you were stunned by the color of his skin, the way it glowed and pulsated, and you wanted to tell him that he shouldn't stand out there in the street unprotected. He should stay inside the TV, where he would be more safe.

Black and white was its own life-form, its own universe. It was the opposite of high definition, virtual reality. Each time the blood-brain barrier was breached, each time black and white broke out into color, you experienced the shock all over again. *The Wizard of Oz*, of course, Kansans turning into munchkins, but also the first color TVs in the homes of your more affluent classmates. How proud they were, how less-than you felt as they demonstrated the art of turning the knob to adjust the garish color just so. It's not the same now when you catch *Casablanca* or *The Maltese Falcon* on the movie channel. Black and white is an antique now, quaint, like milk in glass bottles. It's no longer a shared alternate reality. And that everyday black and white reality that was always there when you were a child is lost forever in the archives where Buster Keaton and Ernie Kovacs sleep in alphabetical proximity.

People who grew up in black and white still carry its aftertaste. You're thinking especially of your sister, who was born in 1935, and had her tired, old, anemic blood drained out and replaced with someone else's blood just last week. You suppose it would be best if they transfused her with healthy, young, Technicolor blood, but you hate to think that she's been colorized. You want her to inhabit the noir. You want her to have Bette Davis eyes. Especially now, in the dark gloom of this post-election season of weeping, the absence of color seems right, as if the whole country wanted to wear funeral black, veils over the face to keep from seeing the unthinkable, and white gloves to keep from touching the filth. You don't want to go out into the world of serial predation and gun massacres in a red dress. You want to lurk in the shadows in the back of the balcony, and if the going gets really tough, you want to alleviate the pain with some vintage goofiness. Chaplin, Harpo Marx, something in black and white that speaks to the absolute absurdity of this life.

Living Arrangements

YOU have no interest in my mother. Why should you? She was not a headliner. She was not noteworthy outside the family and our immediate neighborhood on the Upper West Side. There she induced a certain energy field, like minor royalty, a second cousin of a third-tier baroness. Her generation long gone, there are only a handful of people left who remember her powdered face, chalk white with pink circles of rouge on her cheeks and cerulean smudges on her eyelids, the seams on her stockings almost straight. How remarkable, then, that DNA dictates that her ghost has now moved its furnishings into my body. It's an almost perfect fit, my osteoporotic spine bending to accommodate hers, my thighs expanding to make room for her ample shape. I keep my used Kleenex in the waistband of my pants as she did, and have recently elected to wear my hair parted on the left with a jaunty wave over my right eye. Caroline, expertly wielding the comb and scissors, comments that it has a twenties look, and, sure enough, there is my mother's marcelled cut from long before I was born coming into focus in the salon mirror.

Once, about five years before she died in 2006, I broke down in tears in Great Barrington when she suffered an excruciating compression fracture far away in California. Feeling helpless and anguished, it suddenly became clear to me that she had been my first home, that there was a time in 1945 when I lived inside of her in a warm, dark, wet tenement that she carried around with her when she squeezed the melons at the fruit stand and picked out a seeded rye at the bakery on upper Broadway. Of course, being well into my fifties, I knew all about gestation. But somehow I had always given more thought to my own pregnancy, my own motherhood. This moment of recognition near the turning of the millennium was a first encounter with my deep origins in the swampy folds of my mother's flesh.

The image is like a bellows, expanding and contracting, inflaming memory. Sometimes the fire is reduced to embers. The long years of adolescence and early adulthood when I didn't want any part of her. The bitter winter in my garden where her ashes are now resting, for the most part unattended. I thought when I buried them there that she and I would chat regularly about the anemones, about the grandchildren, about the unrelenting passage of time. But words don't seem to be the medium of our exchange. She speaks to me through my short legs and misshapen feet, my pale blue lashless eyes. She inhabits me as I inhabited her seventy years ago. And she keeps me company. She is there in every gesture. When I throw back my head to wash down a pill. When I drink my coffee out of a thin porcelain cup. I have grown up and drink it black now, not light and sweet with nondairy creamer and saccharine as she did. But I am still married to the aristocratic pinkie lift that I must have learned at her linen-covered dining room table.

My father was morbidly sentimental. You couldn't go to a matinee with him without the crumpled handkerchief coming out of his pants pocket to dry the tears that fell at every cinematic loss or betrayal. But my mother was ensconced in her corset and devoted to decorum. When she was hurt or angry, she would take to her bed. When she felt the need to cry, she would leave the room. She couldn't bear the exposure of open grieving or gratitude, retreating to the kitchen while my sister's husband, only sixty, lay dying. Hiding in a dark corner of a back room while her circle of friends and family celebrated her birthday with rounds of rye and ginger. Now, traveling as she is inside of my life, wandering through my days along the highway of hyperawareness, on the far side of several personal and historical upheavals, she cries openly all the time. It is my gift to her.

Paleolithic Father's Day

My mother and father slept in separate beds. Between them, a stack of detective novels and crossword puzzle books teetered on the night table. In the morning, my father would sit on the edge of his bed, fish around for his slippers, and shuffle into the kitchen where my mother was boiling water for the instant Maxwell House, mixing the Minute Maid, and tearing apart English muffins. Never cut an English muffin. Once he settled in at the kitchen table, he turned on the crackly transistor radio. He had gone all the way with Adlai back in '52, but most Americans liked Ike and some even had a soft spot for Joe McCarthy. It was best to keep your head down, go to the shop, come home from the shop, eat your dinner, and watch *Father Knows Best,* though he could hardly identify with the clean-shaven, suburban protagonist, and certainly not with the sentiment conveyed by the title. When I think about my father, the pendulum of my memories swings from affection to discomfort and back again. He was a decent man, but his animal nature, his essential wildness was somehow attenuated, left behind in a remote corner of a prehistoric past life.

While he listened to the news, my mother would lay out his clothes—boxers, sleeveless undershirt, trousers, belt, shirt freshly pressed at the Chinese laundry, tie and tie clip, sports jacket, socks, and cordovans. She bought and dispensed all of his clothes. He did not say, "I feel like wearing the green tie today." She managed his wardrobe like a pitching rotation, varying only in the event of injury, a spot of pot-roast gravy on the scheduled tie. In the wall-to-wall mid-century malaise of the apartment on upper Broadway, there was no room for Daddy. Everything had its place. Dinner at six.

My father didn't drive. A few times a year on a Sunday holiday—could be Father's Day—Uncle Jerry or Uncle Leo would chauffeur us in a two-tone Chevy and head north and west, crossing the George Washington Bridge into the untamed wilderness of Englewood or Nyack, where people had basketball hoops attached to the sides of their garages and barbecues for roasting marshmallows and kosher hot dogs. In the kitchens, resplendent with breakfast nooks and the glossy patina of waxed linoleum, the women would arrange bowls of potato salad and dishes of pickles, while in the backyards the children swatted at mosquitoes and the men tended the fire. You could see my father, eyes watering from some combination of smoke and wistfulness, staring into the blaze like Paleolithic man the day he first discovered the sorcery of rubbing two sticks together. Pinochle games would come and go. Someone would have a second drink and tell a very bad old joke, salacious enough to induce smirking but obscure enough to leave the children bewildered. Someone else would make a thinly veiled racist remark. And still my father would be staring at the fire.

His fixed gaze left you wondering what he was looking at in there. Some vision of the hunt, a large carnivorous animal tramping around in the brush while he, Sidney Rosenberg, stands behind a leafy tree, waiting for just the right moment to hurl a rock that fells his prey and provides the family dinner. There he is in Bergen County with his hands clasped behind him, rocking back and forth on his heels, the blood in his veins mingling with the dimly remembered blood of a creature he would eat, the smell of the flesh rising to his nostrils with the grilling Hebrew National franks. He sees his haunches draped in the skins of some previously slaughtered beast. He is close to them, the animals, eating them, wearing them. Always on the lookout, his vision and hearing sharp, penetrating the deep silence of the forest, not overwhelmed by the wailing of sirens on the avenue, the constant burbling of the television. After all, the survival of the family depends on his acuity, his speed and strength. He is his most authentic self singeing his eyebrows in front of the fire. Then, with regret, as the light begins to fade in some cousin's backyard, my father drags himself away from the embers and submits to Manhattan, a short man engulfed by tall buildings.

Going Home

SHE is making a hajj, a holy pilgrimage to the Upper West Side. The buildings she remembers on upper Broadway, each one more baroque than the last, an architectural costume party along the avenue, are for the most part still standing. But the storefronts have all been Gapped and Starbucked beyond recognition. There is one familiar ladies' lingerie holdout, where her mother used to allow other short, ample women to stuff the sausage meat of her flesh into boned and laced casing. And, of course, there is Zabar's, the corner grocery of her girlhood, now a vast museum of consumption, the Uffizi of food.

From the window of her father's antique store at 2244 Broadway, you could look directly across the street into Zabar's and marvel at the expert slicing of sturgeon. Now the great theft-inviting window of her father's store, once filled with cloisonné, sterling, and lace, is gone. For a while in the eighties, there had been a shop displaying improbably pointy Italian footwear in the window at 2244, but now only the numbers remain over the door. They are selling overpriced real estate in there.

Continuing uptown, she turns left on Eighty-second to have a look at her old school, PS 9. The Victorian structure was outmoded in the fifties and later went through a period of abandonment, dark and hollow-eyed. Now, during the Bloomberg revival of Gotham self-importance, it has been repurposed and renamed the Mickey Mantle School. She goes in and stops at the front desk to ask about the rolling-door classrooms. Do they still have them? Entire floors of the five-story building, one huge open space, decorated with a plaid of tracks on the floor that allowed the space to be divided into classrooms. On Friday mornings the doors were rolled back for assembly, "One nation under God," even the Lord's Prayer. On all the other days, the submissive children of the Eisenhower era sit silently with perfect posture, listening to one teacher hold forth on Paul Revere's ride while another explains fractions. No need for soundproofing between classrooms. Self-expression is frowned upon. One clerk smirks knowingly at another when she asks about the rolling doors. Once a month or so, someone of her vintage gets that look in her eye, asks this question. The rolling doors are dead and gone, as are some of the children.

There is a very young Russian wearing an imposing coat at the door of her building opposite the multiplex on Eighty-third Street. He is bewildered by the reverential soft-shoe she does on the granite threshold and the little, almost sexual, squeals she makes when she actually sets foot in the mock-baronial lobby, taking in the marble flooring, the blinding brass of all the trim, the mirrored doors. "I lived here from 1945 to 1967," she tells him, feeling at once very important, very old, and dimly aware that his parents were probably being ground into the steppe by Stalin in 1945. Or maybe it was his grandparents and maybe she is historically hyperactive. It has always been so with her, this sharing of space with the past as with an occupying army. It takes over the best houses and eats all the food. Her nostrils are still filled with the smell of her mother, an amalgam of underwear, instant coffee, and crepe de Chine.

This piece of turf, the cracked sidewalks, the sycamores, the gargoyles craning their necks out of the eaves of the buildings, is somehow hers and not hers. It's not just the new storefronts and the evidence of wealth in the displays and on the window shoppers. It's not just what has been added. It's what's missing. Her mother is missing. She shriveled up inside the cage of her nursing-home bed in California, taking with her the ten-year-old who knitted socks for the soldiers in the Great War; the glamorous, slender party girl of the twenties with a dance card the length of a scroll; and the jazz age ingenue who batted her eyelashes when she had too much to drink. She took the imperious, rotund mother of the forties and fifties and the anxious wife of the sixties and seventies, spending her days with her ailing husband in the waiting rooms of oncologists. She took the old woman, driven to fat by an intractable Hershey Bar habit and to confusion by a seizure condition that made her stop mid-sentence and stare into the distant nothingness. And then, finally, one day, waiting for the elevator in the carpeted hallway of a senior-housing facility, a sharp noise startled her and caused her to turn abruptly and lose her balance, and she fell to the floor and into the tunnel that led to another kind of home.

Acceleration

IMAGINE the fall of the French monarchy at the end of the eighteenth century. Blood trickling down the cobblestone streets, heads in powdered wigs toppling like melons from the apex of a pyramid of produce. On this side of the Atlantic, no one would know about it for weeks, maybe months, as news drifted languorously across the ocean with the fickle winds. The captain of a sailing vessel idly mentions to his first mate that he has heard murmurings about a Corsican of short stature whose influence is on the rise in Paris. After the ship docks in Boston, a pre-industrial game of telephone ensues, so that people in Hartford hear that a Sicilian midget is waiting in the imperial wings. By the time the rumor reaches New York, the upstart has become a short-haired Maltese, causing some people in New Jersey to hold fast to the belief that the new emperor of the French will be a cat. News of events beyond the salons of Europe never reaches America at all, the only thing entering the country from southern latitudes being microorganisms nesting comfortably in the fetid clothing of sailors, much like their swine-flu descendants, only at a more leisurely pace. Information is power. No one knows anything.

Now along comes the nineteenth century, with the mournful aria of the train whistle keening across the empty prairie over the percussion of the locomotive clacking along the tracks. News of the California gold rush travels fast enough to stimulate the salivary glands of bankers in New York. Steamboats on the Mississippi bring cotton upriver and slaves downriver, each one with his own story, her own song. In this way, the pain and the stain spread like red dye in a load of white laundry. Crusading journalists seize the opportunity to mold public opinion. People who have the advantage of literacy swallow newspapers with their morning pancakes. They argue fervently about abolition, about the Union, about the future of the young country. The telegraph and the transatlantic cable drive the pace of information, now mechanized and encoded for the first time into dots and dashes. A certain distancing creeps in. The French and the Germans are fighting again. What else is new?

Still, the excitement of sharing the story is spreading, and the tempo is picking up. Promenading above the scramble for bread there is a class of people with access to an instrument that can be held up to the ear and mouth, enabling the miracle of disembodied conversation. Lives are saved. Gossip travels more rapidly across town. A box on the kitchen table sings to you and transports you across the miles to the scene of sporting events. In short order, the box replaces the table itself as the altar of family life. On the ground, horses are put out to pasture as more and more people are swept up in the erotic energy of the automobile. It takes you where you want to go. It knows no boundaries, save the water's edge. You can have sex in the backseat. And if that's not enough speed, soon you will cruise over the grid of cornfields and dairy farms of the American heartland and at night over the glittering electrified cities below. Soon every town will have its Bijou or Roxy, where people more beautiful than we are will hold sway in the dark, all eyes fixated on their exceptional faces, all hands mining for pleasure in the adjoining seat, all mouths struggling to breathe in the desire-drenched air. After the Second World War, which some of our fathers fought in or nearly starved in, there will be television; and soon there will be images of maimed soldiers and refugee marches and orphaned Asian children in your living room on your Zenith. There will be more information, but also more disinformation, more merchandising, more fantasy, more self-doubt.

But all this is only the preamble to the torrent of data that will come when the entire country, indeed the entire world, becomes enmeshed in a web of bits and bytes arriving simultaneously from all directions, all of us gleefully interconnected all the time to the global anxiety of the twenty-four-hour news cycle, the worldwide pornography market, the opportunities to make money or lose money at spectacular speed, the images, the videos, the tweets. Information is power, but is it oxygen? Can you breathe it?

Now, blood again, everywhere. Brown blood, white blood, black blood, all red. People in ugly Christmas sweaters stuffing cookies in their mouths, gunned down by Tashfeen, our first A-list mass shooter who is also a mother. Tashfeen and Syed, rampaging out of the southern California nowhere with their arsenal of semiautomatics. Video cameras scanning the horizon, documenting rafts stacked with bodies sinking in the freezing Adriatic. A caliphate rising out of the rubble as xenophobic Europeans close their borders to refugees and nativist Americans work to disinfect our country from the perceived Muslim infestation. Screaming, fear mongering, chest thumping like drunken football fans, all of them. Giant Macy's parade inflated balloons of ISIS jihadis, Trump, Assad, Putin—all pumped full of testosterone, hovering above the desperate, the hungry. Everyone who is anyone macho posturing. Oceans rising, drought advancing, whole species vanishing. Ukraine not even worth a few column inches. Black men executed in the street. Guns in every kitchen cabinet, cuddling up to cornflakes. Life is cheap, and even we who were born lucky into white America are drowning in the dystopian deep end, and a lot faster than we were before. Is it possible to dam up the river of incoming information for just a week, a day, to shoot the shit instead of one another, to talk about nothing much?

Tragedy in the Tropics

LAST night I found myself dreaming about Puerto Rico. I saw the cars lining up, the babies screaming, and the long, dark, suffocating nights. I saw the beaches, the jungle, El Yunque, the colonial architecture of San Juan, and the children of the Puerto Rican diaspora I went to school with sixty-five years ago. They are homeless now, the families of these children. They are thirsty. My dreams are indistinguishable from the reporting coming in from the island. I see the catastrophe when I lie down and when I rise up.

The boundary of the Puerto Rican community on the Upper West Side of Manhattan began a few feet east of my front door off Broadway, extending all the way to Central Park and along Amsterdam and Columbus Avenues, not yet gentrified. I somehow learned not to walk on those streets, past the bodegas and the places that sold *cuchifritos,* except in a literary emergency if I had to go to the library on Eighty-first Street. No one taught me that lesson. I learned indirectly through gestures, through facial expressions, to be afraid of Otherness, of loud dance music blaring out of transistor radios in the street, of men playing dominoes out on the stoops. In school, the classrooms were as segregated as the ones in Little Rock. A handful were reserved for Us, the well-fed, white-skinned children of the professional and business classes. The remainder of the building consisted of rooms full of Them, children being told not to speak their native Spanish. Recently, in a sorry attempt to make amends, I experimented with a reversal of fortune, trying to study Spanish at seventysomething. No dice. There is no space left in my aging brain that can accommodate verbs in the conditional. It is painful when you can't express yourself. It is painful when people don't understand you. The sisters, cousins, children, and grandchildren of the people I went to school with, trapped on a tropical island dismembered by nature run amok, are hungry now, and will be literally powerless for six months. I try to take it in, this bankrupting, this third-worlding of a part of America. And while I'm trying to digest it, feeling increasingly lightheaded with despair, the man reputedly in charge is tweeting away, accusing Puerto Ricans of expecting too much, of not being willing to help themselves. The catastrophe in Puerto Rico has vacuumed up all the other issues crowding my awareness. The people in Ponce and Arecibo, always, of course, real to themselves, are now real to me. Fear kept me from hearing them when I was a child, but I hear them now, and they are crying out for help.

All lives are finite, but now the finitude of my own life is more apparent to me than it was even ten years ago. The only way to get from today to tomorrow in one piece is by making some decisions about what's most important, performing some kind of reluctant triage. This witness demands that I filter out much of the other incoming noise, the brass band of the political circus blaring oom-pah music at a deafening volume, the lion tamer cracking his whip. We all need to take care of ourselves, stay connected, and stay healthy. But the extent of my concern for the people around me has narrowed, even as it has deepened. I can't allow everyone in. Sometimes, mea culpa, I turn into the dog-food aisle, even though I don't have a dog, just to avoid talking to a perfectly good person I recognize in the cereal aisle. But once I get there, I find that it is covered with hurricane debris and fallen coconut palms. Puerto Rico has not gone away.

In Tobago

ALONG the endless stretch of sand that separated the Turtle Beach Hotel from the turquoise Caribbean, women in bikinis—mostly from Uppsala and Wiesbaden—basted themselves in a glaze of sunblock against the equatorial rays. Most mornings, a group of men would be tugging on one of the nets on the beach. You could see them pulling, leaning back at a forty-five-degree angle, every sculptured part of them straining against the weight of the catch. Finally, with a lot of yelling and gesticulating, the net would be dragged onto the beach. In the hand-tied skein, thousands of jacks, snits, and the occasional shark or barracuda fought for their lives. Women from Plymouth and Black Rock would appear out of nowhere, and the divvying up would begin. There seemed to be a system, but she was damned if she knew what it was. In the end, Wilford, the captain of the net, would walk off with the biggest fish to sell to the hotels, and everyone else would get their share for dinner. There was fish, and there were mangoes. There was breadfruit and mauby and salt cod.

They came to Tobago after her father died. They had gone down to the city to see her mother, who now had little episodes of blankness where she suddenly stopped talking and stared into space. Moments of time went missing so that over all, even though the old lady looked well and performed all the basic walking and talking functions adequately, she was being shaved down from a full-length pencil into one of those little stubs that her father had so loved to collect. It was winter. Colder on the thermometer in

Massachusetts but more miserable in the city in the asphalt chill between the glowering buildings. They desperately needed nakedness, tropical heat, low-grade reading material. They needed to get away from the cold and from the fear of what was happening to her mother.

Between JFK and Piarco Airport in Trinidad, they sat in the sealed capsule reading magazines, drinking gin and tonics, eating what someone had fiendishly called chicken cordon bleu, nodding out for a few minutes, until finally the plane touched down. Inside the airport they were met by an explosion of color and shouting in a mixed West and East Indian patois. Descendants of the Indian indentured servants who replaced the Africans after emancipation crowded the lounge in saris and dhotis and turbans. Everyone was eating roti filled with goat or dal. Carnival was three weeks away, so the soundtrack was blasting rival calypso artists. The two of them were a long way from gray, slushy New England, and in spite of travel fatigue, they were pumped.

The next morning, they took the thirty-minute flight to Tobago and started to breathe. What was the smell of the place? Bougainvillea and coconut, rum punch and curry, and burning garbage. Just driving from the airport at Crown Point to the Turtle Beach, where the taxi driver had decided they were going to stay, she felt a sweet languor descending, wrapping itself around her. A boy was caring for some goats. A large grandma in the headdress of the Baptist women was rubbing a shirt against a washboard. Pairs of girls in cornrows, wearing the dark blue jumpers and starched white shirts of the Anglican uniform, walked home from school. Men placed bets at the "Play Whe" windows, putting the local currency, TTs, down on the same numbers their fathers and grandfathers had played.

Immediately abutting the hotel was the taxi shack where the drivers congregated and played rummy, waiting for fares; and behind that the fish shack, where the men who pulled the nets cleaned the fish, took showers, and smoked Broadways or du Mauriers. During the day, Wilford was generally in the fish shack when there was a catch and playing cards with the drivers when there wasn't.

At night he occupied a barstool, nursed a Carib, and watched the women from under the peak of his cap, pulled way down over his heavy-lidded eyes. Wilford checked out the European fruit as it arrived, wan and weary from travel, then gave it a few days to ripen in the sun. He was patient, philosophical even. Everyone in Tobago had a street name. Wilford was called The Professor.

Coming and Going

"London isn't what it used to be." "Oh my word, no. People are afraid of each other," said the husband, his monstrous camera hanging from his neck. "It's wonderful here in America. Nancy and I love Cape Cod, don't we, duck? I even got a good shot of a great white shark. Just the dorsal fin, of course."

Marjorie recalled that the sign had said the waters off Herring Cove were shark infested. The sharks preyed on the seals. She and Peter had seen the seals swimming parallel to the shore, very close in. They must be skittish, she thought. Like English people riding the Tube late at night, hemmed in by the residue of empire. She remembered how they had walked in the great city, near Piccadilly, trying to identify the languages spoken by women in saris, turbaned men talking into their phones. Urdu, Bengali, their alphabets decorative, each letter its own universe. London was like an animated atlas, the original sound cloud.

Here, at the beach, all they heard were gulls overhead, the slapping of the surf. It was such an immense space. Not a space really, more like an expanse. Behind them, the scrub and rose hips. Under, to each side, and in front of them, the sand dotted with shells, salmon-colored, pale green, mother-of-pearl. Facing them, the sea, stretching to the horizon, beyond which people in pubs, black, brown and white, were drinking their pints. The sky above was the color of cornflowers, the October sun resilient and proud of itself.

Marjorie thought of the offhand remark of the English woman, casually dropping snarky social commentary into the otherwise perfect afternoon, like a pebble disturbing the glassy surface of a lake. Fear. Fear will do that. She remembered an earlier trip to Europe, before she had even met Peter. She had only just arrived from New York, her city-girl instinct for self-preservation still fine-tuned. It was early December. Traveling alone on the train from Stockholm to Uppsala, she picked up a magazine and a container of coffee and settled down in an unoccupied compartment. Doing the Continental, sitting behind the closed door of a railway compartment, watching the flat Swedish scenery out of the smudged window. Marjorie leaned back into a vintage movie fantasy, something Cary Grant-ish. Then the door opened and a man entered the little room. He wore a dull brown wool jacket. He was gray, not his hair, which was straw-colored, but his actual lined and pocked skin. Two watery blue eyes made fleeting contact with hers. The man was carrying a brown paper bag, maybe a bottle of aquavit. Marjorie buried her head in her magazine and took a sip of coffee. After a few minutes, she felt his hand grazing her knee. The unexpected touch rampaged through her like an electric shock. She jumped to her feet and spilled the scalding coffee all over her skirt.

"*Pepparkakor?*" he asked, taking his hand out of the bag and offering her a gingersnap, traditionally served during the Christmas season in Sweden.

"I hate fucking tourists," Peter said, brushing the crumbs out of his beard from the sweet potato *trutas* they had picked up at the Portuguese Bakery. "They're the real sharks. The real invasive species."

"Look," Marjorie pointed. "There's another seal." She wondered if they would flipper up onto the beach if she and Peter weren't there, sprawled on the sand with their Kindles and their water bottles. Someone is always moving in on someone else's turf, redefining the rules of the road.

Marjorie thought, if you took the long view, all of human history, not to mention the sorry saga of our activity in nature, could be boiled down to people pushing ahead on line, elbowing each other out of the way. It was either people from somewhere else with less money moving into the neighborhood, looking dangerously different and depressing real estate values, or, alternatively, people with more money, waltzing up the produce aisle in country-weekend designer clothes, making an ordinary head of lettuce a major investment. It was either pesticides going after bees and butterflies or deer showing up in suburban supermarket parking lots.

"We're all just passing through. We're all migrants," Marjorie offered in her standard fortune cookie style. This was the wide-angle lens she tended to use when considering the larger questions.

"Not me," Peter said, lying back on the towel they had lifted years ago from a hotel in the Caribbean and zooming in on the moment. "I've got my ass on the beach and my face in the sun, and I'm not going anywhere."

Roll Over Beethoven

WHEN John Lennon was shot in 1980, I had a dream that he was sitting in a circle in heaven with my father and my Uncle Jerry, two fabulous, small Jews who had only just died in the late seventies. He seemed to be giving them some valuable pointers about how to get along in the new neighborhood. Mind you, I don't believe in heaven in the angels-with-harps sense of the word, but there he was with one mustachioed New Yorker on either side of him, holding each by the hand and oming away. It was a great comfort to know that my father, a nonbeliever, and my uncle, a conventional shul-on-Yom-Kippur Jew, would be supervised in the world-to-come by someone with spiritual chops. I'm thinking about John because just recently Chuck Berry and Jimmy Breslin left us, and it reminds me that the older you get, seventysomething in my case, the more you experience celebrity loss as well as personal loss. The people who have most impressed themselves on my awareness are at least as old as I am and are, in the nature of things, shriveling and dying off like garden lettuce in mid-summer.

It's always noteworthy when two famous figures die within a few days of each another. It causes a shift in the planetary angle of inclination. Certainly, Carrie and Debbie had that effect. Or Robert Mitchum, the compelling noir actor, whose obituary was vacuumed off the page by Jimmy Stewart, who died the next day. The public can only digest one forkful of nostalgia at any given time. At the moment, I imagine Chuck and Jimmy in some smoke-filled celestial backroom, chomping on cigars and telling outrageous, self-aggrandizing stories. I don't know if Chuck Berry was aware of Jimmy Breslin, but you have to think that Jimmy appreciated Berry's high-wire act on the guitar. Celebrity deaths have the same magnetic intensity as unexpected celebrity encounters in life. I once saw Muhammad Ali walking down Seventh Avenue. Not only was he the most enormous person I had ever seen, but the wavelengths he radiated didn't seem to belong to the normal visible spectrum. He was literally larger than life.

Ordinary, finite beings like us are fascinated by death because it's where we go to play catch with the infinite. Otherwise, we have to settle for contemplative practices and certain chemicals that give us a taste of the vast boundlessness from which we came and to which we will all return. But most people sober up the next morning and go to work or the dentist. Life on this plane imposes a great many demands. Because we don't have the luxury of time to consider death as a philosophical construct, our ideas remain under-cooked and tough from the urgency of fear.

People seem to think of themselves as separate units of consciousness and death as something wholly other, a complete departure from life that comes at the end, in the bottom of the ninth. This is the temporal equivalent of flat-earth theory, which is enjoying a comeback. You just keep going until you fall off the edge. The story I tell myself is different. I imagine one all-encompassing, integrated web of life and death with colors and forms transmuting in and out of elaborate designs. Strawberries and tigers come and go. Birds, friends, mothers, rock musicians, and journalists. I saw this in another dream some years ago. I'm standing in the middle of a field, and all the people I have ever known are flowing past me from the right and from the left, like a complex traffic pattern. They keep gracefully arriving and departing. They keep sprinkling me with the fairy dust of their natures. I am the hub of this particular wheel, one of an infinite number of wheels. I am also ephemeral, like you, like all the people coming and going in the dream. Like Chuck Berry's last squealing guitar riff. But the reverberations of that insistent sound, the bridge that it builds out of Beethoven and over the troubled water will go on and on. *Moonlight* Sonata, meet "Maybellene."

Witness

It's like a seven-layer cake, this family. When you dig in with the side of a three-tined silver fork, you get a dark glaze of ganache, a dry floury sheet, then sticky raspberry and apricot. No layer of the family story can be skipped over if the cake in its entirety is to be savored deeply. Its origins in the Balkans. Its shopkeeper livelihood uptown in the big city. The two daughters, a half generation apart. The older daughter's three children, grown to adulthood in the East Bay. One quiet, cautious. One radiant, diffuse. One wounded, craving.

"I want to talk about the family," the older sister asks the younger, visiting from back East.

"OK. Sure. Who do you want to talk about?"

"I want to know how they all died . . . Aunt Julie, Aunt Honey, Uncle Jerry, all of them," she demands with some urgency. She's doing research, collecting data about the end-times of relatives, most of them not all that interesting when they were alive.

My big sister is celebrating her eighty-first birthday, not very old for most people these days, but she got old young. Vascular dementia, I think, though she doesn't seem to have a diagnosis. She naps on the couch when she's not eating and shuffles, right hand on her cane, left hand gripping the piano, the sink, when she moves around her cramped apartment in the basement of the house where she raised her children. Accumulations of twenty-year-old issues of the *Nation* and sheet music from the forties, Rodgers and Hart, Cole Porter, pile up on the floor, making navigation treacherous. Every year, it diminishes. The tempo of her living, the square footage she is willing to move through. She will not go out to commune with the nasturtium in the sun-drenched North Berkeley backyard. She prefers the moldy, dark, familiar confines of her apartment. It suits her.

"You didn't tell me how mother died. Why didn't anyone tell me?"

As it happens, she was there when our mother took her last breath in a nursing home at the age of ninety-nine, but she doesn't remember; and if you press her to respond to a question that she doesn't know the answer to, she becomes irritable.

"Do we have to talk about that now?" she grouches. Still, I'm patting myself on the back, overflowing with self-congratulation. The kind that comes from the perception of devotion, openness, and generosity to a loved one in trouble. I think I'm the only one she can ask about family members long gone. I'm her link to the past. Without me, she can't really heal the wounds that are still festering. Me me me.

She wants to talk about her long-standing hostile feelings toward our mother. I have heard this song before, all my life, but I never really learned the lyrics. She was ten when I was born, so I missed the tone of her childhood, the key to our mother's limited interest in children. I ask if there was anyone else she felt close to when she was young.

"Aunt Julie was always friendly," she says. "But then one day—I can remember it exactly—we were sitting on the gold brocade sofa in the living room, and I was telling her how mean mother was, but she betrayed me. Aunt Julie betrayed me. She acted like she cared, but then she didn't take my side. She went and told on me. After that, mother didn't talk to me for days. She put on that Empress of All the Russias face, you know the one I mean, and just waltzed right by me while I was playing jacks on the kitchen linoleum."

I cherish the story I've invented that my mother and sister resolved their differences at the end. I mean, I really need to believe that. Even if it's not true. Even though I know whatever my sister wants to hang onto is hers to keep, like an old shirt, stained but comfy. The heaviness of carrying that illusion around starts to interfere with my good intentions, reduces my caregiving to the lowest level of nursiness. I pick up after her. I watch her, eagle-eyed, to make sure she doesn't fall. I demand that she take her pills when I want her to take them. "Yes, mother," she responds to maximum effect.

At her birthday party, we watch vintage slides on a rented carousel projector. My sister is luminous. There she is in the fall of 1958, pregnant with her first baby. She's wearing a raspberry-tinted sweater, almost the identical color to the one she's wearing at the birthday party. In the background, Ella Fitzgerald is singing "Bewitched, Bothered, and Bewildered."

We lean our heads together and sing, "I'm wild again, beguiled again, a simpering, whimpering child again," and we eat cake, lots of cake.

Americana
Written before the 2016 election

SOMETIMES you have to take a vacation. You don't actually have to leave the house to do this particular type of traveling. No packing, no tickets, no delays and cancellations, no sciatica from sitting in the same position on the plane for hours on end. This kind of vacation—let's give ourselves permission to plagiarize Ferlinghetti—is a Coney Island of the mind. It originates in the decision to give it a rest. By it, I mean all the slime of public life in this election year of 2016, as well as Orlando, Istanbul, and Dhaka. I'm thinking of the pictures of children in Caracas standing in front of empty refrigerators, a shelf with one slice of pineapple. I mean the feral right-wing populism spreading like mad-cow disease in our country and throughout Europe. I mean the reality of climate change, right here, right now. To the anguished verse of this dirge, I'm adding a chorus of all the very real life struggles, my own and those of all the people around me, all the people I care about. Today, in the face of all that, I'm singing a different song. I'm going rogue, reinventing myself as a person who is not exquisitely attuned to every ripple of suffering, near and far, making space for celebration. Just for the Fourth of July.

 Understand that growing up in New York in the fifties with the family name Rosenberg, Julius and Ethel in the news every morning, I was not brought up on patriotic overtures. We did not see ourselves as Americans in that fireworks, picnics, and parades kind of way. My mother and father, well spoken and beyond reproach, liberal Democrats by profession, were themselves raised by immigrants and had not yet acquired the full complement of native mannerisms. The next generation, of course, learning its lessons from Hollywood, from Dick and Jane, became more acclimated to the cultural landscape. We became more fully at home in our home. Now I live, literally, in a Norman Rockwell town, Stockbridge, Massachusetts, where the artist lived and used local people as models for his paintings. A cop and a young boy at a lunch counter, a family gathered for Thanksgiving. I know these images are sentimental. I'm not entirely delusional, and I don't buy into American exceptionalism. But just this once, I've decided to make a random list of aspects of life in our country that give me pleasure. Just this once.

I love the oceans, one on each side, framing the prairie and the mountains; the approach on the dunes at Marconi Beach in Wellfleet, where I drag my clammy canvas bag stuffed with towels, sunblock, and those books I look forward to eating for lunch. I am all expectation, advancing along the walkway, rose hips and beach grass growing courageously out of the sand, until I see it, the Atlantic, and it disrupts my breathing. I love the Pacific at Big Sur, more enormous than the imagination, where I went to prepare just before my mother died. The sea stretched endlessly before me beyond the cliffs, and the sky glistened overhead. I felt safe entrusting her to their care, my mother as I remembered her, breasts escaping her skirted floral suit, her hair stuffed into a pink bathing cap. In recent years, I have fallen in love with the Mississippi, doing its Mark Twain thing through the humid Minnesota summer air. Habits being hard to break, I find myself thinking about slave ships and steamboats bringing their human cargo upriver. But I catch myself in the act and wag a finger. Not today.

I'm listening, instead, for the sounds coming up the river and filtering into the aural awareness of people up north and all over the world. Gospel, spirituals, and bluegrass, the indigenous music of the American outback that mothered the blues, jazz, and rock and roll. I'm hearing all the sweaty, raunchy, gravelly, unschooled, un-European music that I listened to and danced to when I was young. Girl groups in slinky, sequined dresses, Martha and the Vandellas at the Apollo, come to mind. This was the soundtrack of our newfound sexuality and the rhythm of protest. We stopped for grilled-cheese sandwiches off the New Jersey Turnpike on the way to the March on Washington in 1963 and put some coins in one of those jukeboxes right over the table so we could hear Little Stevie Wonder do "Fingertips, Part 2." Stevie was 13. I was 18 and teetering on the brink of understanding.

Still, this is a frenetic pace. I need America's pastime, a drowsy ball game to rock me into dreams. I love all forms of baseball: major league at Fenway and Camden Yards and the Oakland Coliseum; vendors tossing bags of peanuts in their shells through the air; minor-league parks like Wahconah in Pittsfield; and especially Little League fields. Watching an eight-year-old take on those ritual moves, fading back to make a catch in the outfield, practicing a menacing batting stance, my optimism is restored. Baseball is a reprieve. When I'm tired, overburdened by pointless suffering that I can't remedy and need to give it a rest, baseball creates just the right level of white noise for a luxurious and unapologetic nap in front of the TV on a holiday afternoon.

Not Yet

THERE is another hostage crisis, and we are all captive. Waiting for the outcome of the political circus, the resolution of our deepest anxieties, much of the country is holding its breath. We are all trying to make it through these last few weeks of not knowing, craning our necks, watching the trapeze artists, the tightrope walker. Everything is up in the air while we wait for the advent of solid ground we can stand on. Ours is not a culture that rewards hovering in the in-between. We abhor ambiguity, the shadows. This is a painfully uncomfortable neither here nor there moment, and we are all in it. Yesterday I saw a drawing at a gallery opening that perfectly reflected this condition. The caption accompanying the drawing said, "The abyss yawns, but it does not sleep." Looking up at the tightrope is dizzying. Looking down into the abyss is frightening. And there is no straight ahead. Not yet.

At home I wrap myself in sweaters and blankets. I eat too much comfort food and watch baseball. It's been raining all day, but not in Chicago, where the Dodgers are playing the Cubs. During the unfolding of the postseason, I think about the rain. It's that rain that always comes when fall begins to lean into winter and the burnt sienna trees give up the ghost. It streams through the porous roof of the sukkah, a monument to impermanence. Here in New England, in the attics of our minds, where we keep the wool socks, the thermal underwear, we are anticipating ice. We don't know it consciously, and we don't know exactly when it will come, but soon enough we'll be standing outside the door sprinkling rock salt like confectioner's sugar down the front steps. But not yet. This is above all a season of not yet.

We have not yet fallen on the ice this year. Later, it will hide on the blacktop or under the snow, threatening us with its slippery lack of empathy. Sometimes it will fall from a dark sky and cover our windshields with a brittle crust, daring us to get from here to there unharmed. It has its upside, ice does. It offers its slick, glassy surface to swanlike Russian skaters. But overall, ice is misanthropic, unloving. Better to crush it mercilessly and introduce it to margarita.

When it melts in the spring, crocuses giggle, birds trill their free-spirited singsong. Then droplets irrigate the born-again grass, rivers rush headlong to meet the sea. Waves approach the shore, tickling the toes of small children building sand castles with moats that empty and fill with the August tide. Once, long ago, when we were taking our two boys to Tobago for the first time, the airline lost our luggage. We arrived in the punishing heat dressed for the arctic, no sandals, no bathing suits. The very first thing we did was tear off our north-country clothes and fly naked and unashamed into the Caribbean; after which, covered in sweat and salt, we stood rapturously under cascading outdoor showers that reminded us of the waterfall back home where the Konkapot meets the Umpachene. It receives us, water does. It cleanses us and slakes our thirst.

In another state, not red or blue, but scalding hot enough to burn your hand when you drain the angel hair, water becomes steam. It whistles a happy tea tune. It creates an entire percussion section, making that deeply consoling knocking noise that tells you the radiators in a drafty New York apartment love you and won't forget you. It pours out of our mouths in winter breath, affirming for us that we are warm-blooded animals, even as the air on the far side of our skin is below freezing. Water has its moods, icy and forbidding, steamy and evanescent, just right for swimming, for drinking.

Watching the rainfall, a lesson from nature arrives at my front door. It's the lesson of neither here nor there, the understanding that definite boundaries in time and space are often human conventions, designed to make our experience intelligible, tolerable. This, not that. But what if the various material states of water are not bounded, despite everything we learned in school about the boiling point, the freezing point, in Fahrenheit and Celsius? Our teachers admired specificity. They had no feel for those liminal, intermediate moments when water hovers between solid and liquid, liquid and vapor, like an indefinite predawn consciousness between dreaming and waking. This is the existential situation we find ourselves in for another two weeks, waiting for the election to be over. It's foreign to our way in the world. Still, here we are, the future of our country hanging in the balance, inhabiting a state of suspended animation, like water on those days when it freezes, then melts, then freezes again. Or those times when it refuses to boil, no matter how intently you stare at it.

A Pebble of Regret

THE old woman has been sleeping in her lounge chair all day. She wakes up periodically to eat leftover frozen enchiladas, but nods off after noshing and naps luxuriantly unless someone comes down to check on her. Her daughter, so devoted, asks if she needs something to drink, but my sister doesn't respond. She's breathing, but just stares into space and moves her mouth around. No words come out. It may be a ministroke. She's going to need a transfusion of new blood from charitable young people who have red blood cells to spare. She needs, as they say, a new lease on life.

I call her after the procedure to assure myself that she's still my sister, even with the blood of nameless college students and dental assistants flowing in her veins. I tell her that I'm coming to California and will see her on November 16.

"Do you remember what day that is?" I ask, in the infantilizing, self-satisfied tone of someone who already knows the answer to her own question.

"Daddy's birthday," she blurts out with sudden alacrity.

There is something about her saying the word Daddy that fills me with an unaccountable joy. She is, after all, the only person in the world who can say that to me. She is the only other person who had that relationship with our gentle, distracted father, almost forty years gone. It's an album of memory we share, even though we are more than ten years apart. Even though she was a Depression and War baby, and I was a child of the American ascendancy. It was only after he died, during one of those long, gossipy coffee-and-Danish storytelling sessions in the house of mourning, that I discovered that his father, our Budapest-born grandfather Ludwig, had died in 1935, the year my sister was born. I had always thought he died in 1945, the year I was born. I had always thought she had a grandfather I didn't have, the ultimate bigger piece of cake. But, as it turned out, we were both lost girls with no doting grandpa to buy us penny candy. There was comfort in that.

Between the two of us lay an expanse of tumbleweed empty of brothers and sisters, a no-man's-land where there was a family, but I wasn't in it. I have amnesia for a life I never experienced. I can't get a feel for it. FDR, war news, radio. Our parents young and hopeful. She in her Persian lamb jacket. He with his fedora at a rakish angle. My sister learning her long division in the same classrooms of the same school I would much later attend. They seem to have managed just fine without me, and this feeling imparts a yearning and produces a pebble of regret that precipitates out of the joy I feel when I hear "Daddy's birthday." All those birthdays before I was born. Ten years when it was just the three of them.

Some people are worriers, other people regret. Worriers are oriented toward the future and all the dangers that are lurking there, the plane crash, the diagnosis, all the catastrophes to come. We regretters are vulnerable to sadness and self-blame. We are magnetized by the past, the missed opportunities, the cruelties, all the failures already in the bank accruing interest. My husband is inclined toward worry. He sees possible losses driving in his direction on the wrong side of the road, coming for him. I am a regretter by trade. I encounter loss bushwhacking my way through the past. He and I try to meet for morning coffee in the parlor of the present. When he gets too far ahead of himself, I try to call him back to now. When I retreat into an unforgiving black hole of self-recrimination, he invites me back up to the fresh air of this moment before 8:24 becomes 8:25 and I miss the whole thing.

He says, "I got my worry from my mother. Where'd you get your regret?" I say, "I found it all by myself in the empty space between my sister and me, the virgin terrain where there used to be a life I will never know."

The Sunny Side of the Street

OUT of the fog of my childhood, I see my fundamental relationship to the world coming into focus. My witness to the famines, the refugee camps—from the end of World War II to the present—has somehow not altered my essential optimism, however unwarranted it may be. The *American Journal of Epidemiology* reports that this may be good for my health. I'm not sure about that. On the contrary, a tablespoon of harsh reality taken once a day might improve my vision. But, insofar as the *Journal's* prognosis is true, I owe my conviction of well-being to my father. Last week I observed his Yahrzeit on 14 Kislev, the anniversary of his death on the Hebrew calendar. He died on December 14, 1978. This year the Hebrew and secular dates coincided on the fourteenth, which is unusual, but then these are unusual times.

My father was born in New York and raised in the Yorkville section of the city, where German was the predominant language. Too young for WWI and too old for WWII, he came of age in the twenties, with no memory of trench warfare and no capacity to imagine the coming horror. He was an antiques dealer by trade, a clever business person, but also a man with an eye for beautiful things. He bought and sold objects made in Europe that became signifiers of culture to Americans who admired the filigree and gilt, the expert craftsmanship. It was understood that the merchandise in his dusty shop, an allergist's paradise, could not be arranged neatly in shelving and bins like so much underwear at Macy's. The display had to be casually profligate, haphazard, a commotion of cups and saucers. The customer was invited to wade through the stacks of dinner plates and tureens, wandering up and down the aisles, past the Meissen figurines and the Dresden dessert dishes, without a care in the world, without a thought of the real and very recent history of those places. This was the fifties, after all. My mother stood behind the glass showcase gossiping with the customers. My father cruised West End Avenue, doing his best to acquire, at the most advantageous prices, the cherished valuables of widows with goulashy Viennese accents before the wobbly old ladies decamped for Florida. Like a surgeon, he extracted the heirlooms, polishing each piece with care so the old world tarnish would for the most part be removed. Then he resold the porcelain and sterling to shiny Americans, willfully ignorant of history. My father was a gentle, unmarked man. For him, Majdanek was like Aleppo, something observed from a safe distance. Something that happened to someone else.

In our house, we took a sanguine view of things. We voted for Stevenson. We believed our country would one day embrace the Puerto Rican children my father lovingly tutored in English after school and the black people we saw on the IRT local, even the woman who came down from Harlem to clean, hanging her coat on a hook in the back bathroom off the kitchen. We were well intentioned and criminally naive.

In our house, we were convinced that America would win the cold war. That in the end, no country with a vulgarian head of state who banged his shoe on a desk in the sacred confines of the United Nations could come out on top. Poignant, isn't it? 2017 is the centennial of the Russian Revolution. We thought we had disposed of the Russian bear, but here he is again, sniffing around the remains of our picnic. We continue to forage for the lessons of the past century. My father is gone, but I am still processing my grandparents' immigration and assimilation stories, the long journey out of the old world and into the new. We all drag our family stories around with us wherever we go, rarely setting them down long enough to listen to all the other stories. Your ancestors were brought here from West Africa in chains? Generations of the men in your family got their paychecks and their emphysema in the coal mines? It would shock my father and other shopkeepers in New York and Budapest, where his parents were born, to discover that things could go bad, and from there to worse. He provided my mother, my sister, and me a down-market version of the life of the wealthy family in the 1970 Italian movie *The Garden of the Finzi-Continis,* all out on the court dressed in tennis whites when the SS came for them. Like my father, most of us know what we know, and not much else. I have friends whose fathers survived the Holocaust and friends whose fathers were blacklisted. Mine was neither. I am a child of optimism, raised in a household blissfully ignorant of rage and despair. I am at a disadvantage. I have no prior training in catastrophe.

Shattered Glass

SHE is wearing a black-and-purple-striped floor-length caftan made of some velvety material. It is the only thing she owns that really stands up to the Swedish winter, central heating not yet universal in the old buildings in Stockholm. It is also the only article of clothing in her closet capacious enough to house her enormous belly and the person-to-be floating inside of it. How she happened to be on the brink of motherhood in an ice-bound foreign country was a circumstance for which only Lyndon Johnson and Richard Nixon could be held responsible. Her first husband preferred voluntary exile near the Arctic Circle to fighting an obscure third-world equatorial enemy, and she went along for the ride, thumbing her nose at all flag waving, as well as at her family and their dreams of a cozy future.

Now she is living in a crumbling tenement without hot running water on the northern edge of the capital. To get clean, you go to the public baths downtown, a necessary chore that doubles as entertainment. Diversions are few and far between. American deserters are both depressive and hypervigilant by definition. Paranoia is their daily bread. They are a ragtag group of Oklahoma farm boys AWOL from NATO bases in Germany, with a sprinkling of more worldly, college-educated draft resisters, some wanted for stateside criminal actions. Most of them are alone and desperate. Some couple up with Swedish women, and a very few bring their American wives or girlfriends into exile with them. This Christmas

Eve 1971, the woman in the caftan identifies herself as the only pregnant Jewish woman from New York married to a draft resister in all of Scandinavia.

To pass the time and exercise her paltry Swedish, she pours a glass of water and settles down with the local paper, *Svenska Dagbladet*. The usual xenophobia about Turkish and North African guest workers hijacking blue collar jobs and Soviet émigrés elbowing native doctors out of line. The Swedes are so proud of themselves with their neutrality and their much-vaunted orderly socialist experiment. But really, scratch the surface, and there it is, the same shit. It is a poor excuse for a world that she is bringing her baby into. Back in New York, she barely escaped hard hats armed with hammers rampaging through the narrow caverns of the financial district, chasing her and her fellow antiwar demonstrators. But here in Sweden, where this time of year the sun rises only long enough for a cup of coffee and lunch on the run, she is surrounded by Mao-spouting self-invented revolutionaries, who have been known to scatter anti-Semitic remarks as casually as pigeon feed. She feels like the Berlin Wall, keeping her aging parents and their infant grandchild from touching one another. What degree of righteous indignation could possibly justify this deprivation she is so ready to inflict on the generation passing and the one to come?

The woman pushes the paper aside and reaches for the water. Outside, the sun has forgotten how to shine, the streets are covered with old snow decorated with dog piss. But inside, a great miracle is about to happen. Just as she extends her hand to pick up the water glass, it shatters spontaneously in the middle of the oak kitchen table, and just as she jumps up and away from the table to avoid the splinters of glass, her water breaks, sending a warm liquid down her legs under the caftan. So this is how it works, she thinks, observing her mammal self at a safe distance with curiosity, gathering the glass shards into the dustpan, and trailing her waters along the floor on the way to the telephone. Improbably, she is about to give birth to a Christmas baby. When he is four months old, she will lay him face up on a card table to be photographed for his passport, and she will take him home to Watergate, to *The Godfather*, to the ongoing war in the jungle. It will be messy in America, loud and contentious, but they will keep house there nonetheless and breathe their dirty native air.

On Children

I'M thinking, as you might imagine, about babies and children. How they sweat when they're sleeping, giving off the hot, sweet breath of life, all of what they are destined to become concentrated in their small forms. How they squeal when something remarkable happens, like a cupcake or a grandpa. How they go around trailing their blankets and bears behind them, and how they come around and climb up onto your lap to visit. How earnest they are, my two-year-old grandson refusing to go out to the motel swimming pool because he was studying the Gideon Bible upside down. They are power plants of love, generating heat and light if they are properly maintained. But if not, if they are left to sleep among strangers in wire cages under aluminum foil and fluorescent bulbs, in places where hugging is strictly forbidden, well, their thermostats run amok. They become either very hot, violent, inconsolable, or very cold, the sort of children who no longer want to be hugged.

When my son was five or six, we went to a large party at a friend's house in Great Barrington in late summer. It was the kind of party in the seventies where the children were wandering, pioneering off the grid, while the grown-ups passed joints around in circles. We did not helicopter in those days. We floated over our families like hot-air balloons. My son came running up to me with his hands cupped in the international sign for amphibian. He had caught a frog. This was a year or two before he gave his heart to the Red Sox and started baking cakes for Carl Yastrzemski's birthday in August, so the frog had his undivided attention that evening. We put him in a shoe box lined with grass and twigs and punched holes in the top of the box. Later, tired and all done for the day, we brought the box home to our house on Pixley Hill in Glendale.

The three of us, my son and I and the frog in his box, went out into the backyard. It was a green heaven of a big, grassy yard, with the house on one side, the garage on the second, the road on the third, and woods in the back. I said to my boy, "We need to let him go back into the woods where he wants to live, so he can be what a frog's supposed to be." His lower lip trembled. He resisted for some minutes while I urged him to be a liberator. Finally, he lifted the lid off the box. The frog jumped out and crouched on the grass, remaining very still. The frog didn't move. "He loves me," my son said, just as his green friend ran off, heading for the woods. It felt so bad and so good.

To be free of incarceration is the right of every child and every frog. Those tiny Guatemalans and Salvadorans have done nothing to deserve their imprisonment. They are in the wrong place at the wrong time. They are in Trump's America, the wrong place to be a brown person, a poor person, an immigrant. They should go back where they came from so that they can be cut down by one of their own, caught in the crossfire of a shoot-out between rival gangs, their homes turned to desert hovels by drought. They have no right to lie around here waiting to die from malnutrition or lack of medical care in our sweet land of liberty. God, who as we all know, is white, male, and full of himself, didn't invite them to the Fourth of July picnic. No strawberry shortcake for you, *chica*, unless maybe you're picking the berries or washing the cake plates. Otherwise, we will give you nothing, less than nothing, not even your own mother. We will make of your young life a cautionary tale so that other desperate people will know their place. We will make of you a test case to see just how far into the filth Americans will allow themselves to be dragged by this pussy-grabbing predator before we stand up and say No! Anyone who has had a child, anyone who has *been* a child must know that this time is now.

Minnesota August

THEY are playing on their iPads, Plants vs. Zombies, Minecraft. They are digging for worms and sorting through their fishing tackle. We gave the older one a tackle box for his birthday, which he's filled with sinkers and lures, some big enough to catch the marlin that probably don't swim in the scummy pond in Powderhorn Park. The boy, my grandson, has shoulder-length hair streaked blond from the sun and mostly in his mouth. Fishing relaxes him. He wants to go to Lake Nokomis to hang out with the adult anglers, Latinos and Hmong, catching their dinner. There is a mostly silent communion among them, free of the racket and posturing he has to deal with around other nine-year-olds. They speak a marine Esperanto. Hooks, weights, bullheads, and crappies. Last winter the boy and his father went ice fishing up north. This is something people in Minnesota do to give shape to the brief hours of daylight during the fierce and interminable winter. They cut a hole in the ice, set up a temporary shelter, and sit there until they can no longer feel their toes. The boy finds this deeply soothing, and he's not even drinking bourbon out of the bottle like everyone else. If you ask him about boats, if he hopes to own one sometime down the road, he says, "Yes, yes I do." And if you ask him what kind of boat he'd like to have, he says, "A one-person kayak."

The boy isn't in Little League like his dad was. He doesn't career effortlessly across the outfield. He doesn't scrape the skin off his knees and shins sliding into second, and he doesn't go out for pizza after the game, win or lose. He is not a team player. There was an older boy, also exceptional or quirky, in the current argot, who used to live next door. After a violent thunderstorm last summer that crushed Fred's house across the way and took down branches all along the street, the two boys went up and down collecting the wood, piling it high, and cutting it up into manageable pieces with handsaws. They had an entrepreneurial commonality. My grandson, not yet eight at the time, had spent the previous winter shoveling snow for the neighbors. He handed out flyers written in crayon and waited for the weather to generate business. Minnesota puts money in the pockets of snow shovelers. But then the older kid moved to another part of town, and the boy was left to his own devices and the company of his professionally sociable younger brother, who knows him as the one who can swim, the one who can read. Together, they form what their father calls an anarchist collective.

  We visit them every year in late August. The days are long at the northern latitude, and the sun beats down on you and your dinner at the picnic table in the backyard. We have a tacit understanding, grandpa, grandma, and the two boys. We all know that our time together is short and that there are certain rituals that must be reenacted, certain memories that must be reinforced. We take the Lake Street Bridge over the Mississippi to the Highland Park pool in Saint Paul, so the little one can splash in the shallows and I can provoke amazement and delight in the older one by going down the two-story waterslide after him. Then we go to Izzy's for cones. An Izzy, for the uninitiated, is a small extra dollop, like a dot on an *i* that sits on top of your cone. While waiting on the sometimes formidably long line, you have to decide on your primary flavor, as well as the flavor of your Izzy. Once served, we sit in the street and get as much ice cream as possible on our faces and our clothes. Finally, we go down the block to Choo Choo Bob's. Just saying Choo Choo Bob makes me happy. Bob, assuming there is such a person, owns a store that is the paradigm of soft sell. There are two or three low-lying train tables in the back, with tracks and engines, bridges and tunnels. At the tables, small children do what small children do, and around the perimeter, young mothers and fathers rest from their labors. No obligation to buy anything. Just an opportunity to witness your young during the waning days of late summer and the fleeting moments of their childhood.

The Empathy Strikes Back

I read in *Real Simple* magazine that empathy is trending. But those streams of people hurtling off the Van Wyck, those pro bono lawyers camping out cross-legged at JFK, that's not a trend, that's a major spike. That's the yeasty conscience of America rising up and saying no. The news will not continue at that exhilarating pace, but something is definitely happening here. The action that some people are taking is lifted up by the empathy bubbling up from a great many more people.

Of course, like hot yoga and the paleo diet, empathy isn't for everyone. In his recent *Tikkun* article "Normalizing Trump's Authoritarianism Is Not an Option," Henry A. Giroux writes that the perpetrators of the invasion of Washington are engaging in "a demented appropriation of Ayn Rand's view that selfishness, war against all competition, and unchecked self-interest are the highest human ideals"; and further, that going forward, "compassion and respect for the other will be viewed with contempt." Up until now, it's been greed that has stumped me, left me shaking my head in bewilderment. How much is enough? How many Lamborghinis can one person drive? But this, this is a new frontier, beyond greed, beyond racism and misogyny, to the core of a Darwinian universe. Not only don't I care about you, but I have nothing but disdain for anyone else who might care about you. It's the twenty-first-century law of the jungle, complete with twittering fiber-optic cables strung from tree to tree.

Everything disseminated from Pennsylvania Avenue can now be traced back to a deep aversion to mercy, considered a symptom of womanish weakness. Preexisting condition? Too bad. Immigrant from the wrong country? Shoulda been born in Omaha. Think you're entitled to free public education? Guess again. Take notice. There will be no more liberal mewling over equity or the plight of the less fortunate. Ridiculing a disabled person is now an acceptable form of theater. From now on, success will be calibrated in units of high-rise real estate and wattage of celebrity. If you don't measure up, your speech will be drowned out by the jingoist brass band, and you will be herded into the stadium to cheer for the all-American winning team. If you don't fall in line, you will be considered not only a loser, but an enemy. The American ambassador to the UN made this clear when she intoned about the expectation that countries will either support any and all U.S. positions or be put on a list. All communication contains an implicit "or else."

But the empathy strikes back. This is because it is fundamental to our humanity, as old as nursing mothers, as ancient as nourishment itself. Anyone who has ever been fed or offered sustenance understands the essential connectivity between people, the hunger to know and to serve. Right now, empathy is coursing through our veins after a consumerist dry spell. Lao-tzu says, "Water is fluid, soft, and yielding. But water will wear away rock, which is rigid and cannot yield." Think of Steve Bannon as a boulder. Think of all of us eroding him until a few gifted and determined people knock him off the precipice.

Empathy is a bio-spiritual condition of being, a process that normally ebbs and flows like desire. It's always there, waiting to be aroused, constantly on the alert for opportunities to replicate, to insinuate itself. Here's how I think it works in the everyday. A seventysomething friend tells me that after a period of uncertainty, she has decided to devote her remaining time to fighting for social justice. I feel the tears welling up in my eyes. This takes place between dance numbers at someone else's seventieth birthday party, and I am taken entirely by surprise. I have forgotten that empathy is the reason that people cry just as much at weddings as they do at funerals. Because it is not only about being willing to see other people's suffering. It is, in the first instance, about recognizing our shared humanity and how much we are alike, warmed by the same sun, breathing the same air. Palestinians in Dearborn breathe. Mexicans in Phoenix breathe. When cowboys in Washington try to round people up like so many farm animals, we all feel fenced in.

These days, empathy is a contagion that has spread rapidly, starting with our smallest private gestures and already resulting in millions of people around the world gathering for the Women's March. It is a flood of human connection, biblical in its proportions, already sweeping the country. There will be no reconstructing the city of indifference. This is how the species survives. This is how the planet survives. Empathy is the foundation of the resistance to tyranny.

On Drowning

WE used to go to Montreal for long weekends, shooting straight up the Northway from Albany and finding ourselves, four hours later, in an actual foreign country. One September we saw Tim Raines, at the end of his illustrious speed-demon career, hit a line-drive double to right field in an Expos 4-2 win over the Phillies, play-by-play in French. We were delirious, despite the anemic size of the crowd and the reprehensible Astroturf. That night we ate a tagine that made us weep for joy; and the following day, a Saturday, we explored the Arab quarter around Rue Saint-Denis and bought our own clay pot so we could re-create the flavor of North Africa in the Berkshires. Montreal felt so international, so open. In an Ethiopian diner, where we went for lunch before making the return trip south, a waitress demonstrated the proper method for eating the spongy bread called *injera* by tearing a piece off the aluminum tray on our table with her hand and stuffing it directly into my mouth. We were lit up when we arrived home late in the evening of September 9, 2001.

Now these neighborhoods and similar areas in London, not to mention Paris and Brussels, seem filled with threat. I am not speaking here of the low probability of being caught in the crossfire or the Eurocentric concern about bombings in familiar places, as against the same bombings in Iraq or Pakistan. I'm not speaking about the origins of radical Islam or the role of the West in aggravating Muslim grievances. I am speaking about the fear that has grown in us over the past several years and the fact that my sense of who I am is offended by this fear. What happened to the person who cherished and defended the idea of a common humanity? Was this person an artifact of a period when the official enemy drank tea from a glass, like my grandma, and trafficked in painted dolls that nested one inside of the other? The cognitive dissonance gives me a headache, and the headache has gotten worse.

It was only five years ago that we spent an afternoon meandering around Brick Lane in east London, inhaling the fragrance of curry and *za'atar*, admiring the Indian women in their pink and green silk saris and the Muslim men in their loose white caftans and *taqiyahs*, indistinguishable to me from the *kippot* worn in synagogue. We were such innocents abroad that we walked up to a group of these men standing outside a small mosque and asked if we could go inside and look around. You know, like tourists. One man asked, "Are you Muslim?"

No, I am not. I am an older American-Jewish woman living in a tranquil preserve in western Massachusetts, far from the current suffering, far from the bombed-out wreckage of Syria, far from the capsized boats crammed with smuggled refugees drowning in the Adriatic. We have seen these pictures, but we have also been assaulted by a constant barrage of fear-mongering images and rhetoric, not only from the usual suspects, but from the empire of entertainment. We have been homelanded.

This year, as I prepare for Passover, my teeth are on edge, filled to capacity with a volatile amalgam of anxiety and sorrow. I consider what it meant to be a stranger in the land of Egypt, what it meant to be enslaved. I picture the Israelites, desperate to be free, rushing toward the sea, and the sea in its turn swallowing the pursuing Egyptians. It is an accident of history that those of us gathering for Seders in the carpeted comfort and apparent safety of our homes, time zones away from the bloodshed, only imagine that we are drowning in our own anguish. It could be otherwise. Sometimes the sea doesn't part, and the drowning is real.

Talk to Me

I pray because it helps me to remember that I'm still here. Much of the time, I am wandering around in my life, daydreaming about missteps in the past or possible pitfalls looming in the future. If I find myself unexpectedly in the present, I am likely focused on explaining the origin of the stain on my skirt to the woman from Ecuador who works at the dry cleaner's or concentrating very hard on cooking the pasta al dente. Prayer happens when I simply notice that I'm alive and spontaneously feel a boundless gratitude for this existential situation that I can't explain. I can't explain life or death. They are equally mysterious. I am just awestruck. To give the experience some shape, I sometimes begin with a prayer formula, like the Hebrew *Baruch atah Adonai*. I say, "Dear God, Holy One of Being, thank you for this day." Other times, I don't speak at all. I simply see pictures in my mind's eye, a place of vision that is not dimming with age.

Lately, I've been reflecting on Psalm 118:24, "This is the day that God made. Let us rejoice and be glad in it." The first phrase comes easily. This is it. This is the day. It will not come again. There is an awareness of mortality folded into "this is the day." Every time I open my eyes to this knowing, I see that my days are numbered. A minor slipup can catapult me out of life and into something else that I cannot be expected to understand. I can be taken by surprise. I can be taken. The Hebrew word *zeh,* or this, is one of God's innumerable names. This and this and this and this. Anguish and babies and elephants and grapefruit. Thunderstorms, Tolstoy, and dog shit. All happening, all renewed in every sacred sunrise.

Like light from a distant star, "Let us rejoice and be glad in it" has only just arrived in my awareness now that I am in my seventies. I am not being called to party, which I was once very good at. I am not being asked to pretend that people in Syria are not being attacked with chemical weapons or that people I love are not suffering. The psalm is suggesting that I remember to rejoice in my aliveness, my witness. Beyond that, it invites me to join in the universal heartbeat. Let us rejoice. For better or for worse, we're all in this together. The witness is collective.

I wasn't brought up with prayer. Like many people, especially people from largely secular Jewish backgrounds, I found the idea of prayer foreign and disquieting. It felt like a form of propaganda designed to disempower me, to transfer my agency to some invisible, elusive, but at the same time all-powerful being outside of myself. Alternatively, I would worry, what if I'm just talking to myself when I think I'm praying? But over time the border between my consciousness and the larger consciousness became porous. I now feel less earnest about prayer, more like a small child humming and telling stories to myself while I draw pictures with crayons or look for pieces to a puzzle. All of us project our individual experience into the collective story that some people call God. We just don't call this prayer. Children understand how the limits of one person can dissolve into the enormity of all there is. When I come to that understanding, I can sing the truth of a particular moment while washing dishes, walking in Stockbridge, drinking cold water on a hot day. Even if the prayer arises out of a sadness in my life, I lose exclusive ownership of it when I share it with all that is listening. The sharing is an act of generosity, a way of saying, here, take this piece of me, even the anxiety and the despair. Let us rejoice and be glad in it.

They Can't Take That Away from Me
November 7, 2016

IF you're anything like me, right about now you feel like everything you hold dear is imperiled. After tomorrow we may be entering a new dispensation in which our president (God forbid) is intimate with both the KKK and the KGB. Your inclination is to focus on those things that give you solace, casting a soft glow on your life, inspiring gratitude, and making you think of drinking Pernod and listening to Edith Piaf. Writing in the second person gives you just the distance you need to escape the black hole of "It can happen here." So you go the second-person route, which you have not done since the very first blog post on *seventysomething*, when you couldn't quite believe you were taking the plunge. You considered calling this piece "These Are a Few of My Favorite Things," but mindful that sentimentality is the flip side of violence, you determined that the treacly Julie Andrews lyric didn't fly. Instead, you went with "They Can't Take That Away from Me," Gershwin's poignant 1937 song. You went to the heart of defiant Jewish New York. The following is a list, hardly exhaustive and in no particular order, of some everyday encounters, all virtually free of charge, that belong to you irrespective of politics and that fill you with tranquility, joy, and amazement. So there.

Drinking coffee in bed. In the indolence of seventysomething, you don't generally rush out of the house in the morning.

Twilight Time

You can make a pot of coffee and pour a cup for yourself (black) and one for Frank (with milk). Then you can get back in bed and read, letting the caffeine work its magic, orbiting other worlds. You can fly to Rome with Jhumpa Lahiri in the pages of *In Other Words*. Watch the remarkable Jhumpa, raised in Bengali and educated in English, as she surrenders to Italian. You can wander with Rabih Alameddine in Yemen, Egypt, and Lebanon and tell him how much you admire his intricate novel *An Unnecessary Woman*. You are hopelessly infatuated with books, like a horny teenager. You can't live without them.

Lemons. You love their astringency, the perfume that floats up from the oil in their peel when it's grated over linguini. Lemons make everything taste better—cod, custard, cocktails. So Mediterranean. You love their color in a blue bowl, definitively yellow, as if nothing else, no daffodil, no sundress could compete. The way they offer themselves up off the tree in your sister's backyard in Berkeley. You are grateful to lemons for their simplicity and their versatility, their willingness to make themselves useful.

Walking in Stockbridge. You never get tired of ambling in disbelief down Main Street, from north of the library, past the Dutch-roofed old town hall, past the gracious Riggs buildings with their charcoal shutters and matte blue doors separating the pain inside from the pain outside, all the way to the cemetery, where your friend Al, a wandering Jew, an interloper, ended up surrounded by legions of church people from old Stockbridge families. Nothing much changes in this town. The trees do what trees are called to do, leafing gracefully in the spring, exploding in cherry blossoms as spring becomes summer, turning pumpkin in autumn, letting go as winter approaches. You feel no need for a different walk. It's less than a mile down and back, but you see something new every day.

Words. English words inhabit your cells in densely populated housing projects. There are so many of them, and each one plays different music. You love their roots in the classical languages, connecting you like ancient Facebook friends to Socrates and Virgil. Sometimes they arrive in steerage or by caravan from the Arab world. Alchemy. Algebra. The history of language defies politics. Eighth-graders in Indiana don't know they're engaging with the mathematics of the Arab world when they struggle to solve equations. They don't know that the word *ojalá*, Spanish for hopefully, comes from the Islamic devotion "If Allah wills it." Words are sneaky. They don't carry passports. They vault over the big wall and set up shop. There are some that irritate and some that terrify, but truthfully, you love almost all of them promiscuously.

You will not be deprived of these pleasures no matter how far the armies of the night advance. You have read the history books, and you know that the struggle to remain who you are in the face of the monster is crucial to survival. In the cacophony of the moment, you wish to make it clear that you will not be bludgeoned.

Trade-In

You know how guys used to trade in the Chevy when it got old for a newer, shinier model? Well, I was thinking maybe there should be a place you could go, sort of like an auto dealership, where you could trade in your life for something faster, with a better sound system. I imagine going in there and meeting Marty, this sleazy salesman in a plaid sports jacket. "Whaddya got for the trade-in?" he asks.

"I got a 72-year-old, smart-ass Jewish intellectual. What can I get for that?"

"Oh, that's a tough one. I got too many of those on the lot already. But wait up a minute. Maybe I can do something for you. Let's see. I can give you a WNBA player, maybe a point guard. Whaddya think? Only thing is, I might have to put you on the rack to stretch you."

"Ixnay. What else have you got?"

"How about something in a foreign model? Maybe a hooker in Singapore?"

"I don't think so. Too much streetwalking in stilettos with pointy toes. Let's be creative. Can I trade for a man?"

"Absolutely. I have a gynecologist just came in this morning. Practically new, right out of medical school."

"OK. Let's have a look." Marty directs me to a prematurely balding, weaselly person with a paunch. "I don't think so. I have to feel a connection. I have to imagine myself out there on the road in that life."

Trade-In

I can see Marty is starting to get really pissed at me. "Look, miss," he says. "What you got for the trade-in, you don't get George Clooney. Know what I mean? Why don't we take a different tack? Why don't you tell me what you're looking for in a life?"

Marty produces two cups of poisonous instant coffee and directs me to an orange plastic seat opposite him at his desk.

"You know, I'm not that sure. It's easy to say what I don't want. I don't want the mayor of Toronto. I don't want Vladimir Putin's girlfriend."

"Never mind the girlfriend. I might be able to get you Putin himself. I got a call yesterday from a colleague of mine, says big, bad Vlad's tired of invading things and shooting planes out of the sky. Wants to settle down in Fort Lauderdale."

"Nah. That's not me. I don't want to be scary. I'm a bit of a people pleaser. I want to be liked."

Marty sighs. "OK. Here's what we're gonna do. I'm gonna say something, and you'll free-associate. Like Freud, know what I mean? Like if I say spinach and you say Popeye, I know you're looking for a regular Joe the Plumber type. But if I say spinach and you say eggs Florentine, then I know we're into something high end, something with real class. You ready?"

"Ready," I say, skeptically.

"Jimmy Durante."

"What?"

"Jimmy Durante. What's the first thing that comes into your mind?"

"Nose."

"Great. You're getting the hang of it. Pinocchio."

"I'm still going with nose."

"Interesting. You could have said puppet or liar, but you said nose again. Let's go in a different direction. What if I say gardenia?"

"Billie Holiday."

"What? What kind of an answer is that? We're talking about a flower here, not a singer."

"Billie always wore gardenias in her hair."

"You know, I'll say one thing for you. You got it right the first time. You are a smart-ass. And why do you suppose she wore gardenias in her hair?"

"Because they smell nice?"

"Yes, yes," Marty yells, pounding on his desk, causing various pink invoices and yellow bills of sale to fly in all directions. "You're obsessed with the nose, with the sense of smell. Let's see what we've got in perfume testers."

"I don't know. Seems kind of elitist. I'd like to have a broader influence. Mass appeal, you see where I'm going with this? Maybe something in TV."

All of a sudden, Marty isn't just pounding on his desk. He's jumping on his desk, screaming, "I've got it! I've got it! Remember how Emeril Lagasse was always carrying on about how good his crayfish smelled or his shrimp étouffée? What a shame it was that the people watching at home didn't have Smell-O-Vision? That's going to be you! You're going to be the genius who invents Smell-O-Vision."

"You can give me that for the used intellectual?"

"Normally, that deal wouldn't fly. But for you, I'm going the extra mile."

Sintra Socks

BEFORE we got to Sintra on the Atlantic, the sky was cobalt every day from sunrise to dusk. That blue against the salmon and dusty rose of the Portuguese stucco was an excitement like biting into a blood orange. It burned your eyes. All over Europe, even across the Mediterranean in Egypt, there was a deep freeze. Snow was falling where snow had never fallen before. But on the Iberian Peninsula, when the crazy climate-change disruption came, it came as rain. The sky went dark over our heads in the village of Elvas in the Alentejo, and we knew we weren't going to get to see the ocean on the coast in Sintra. I had committed the error of anticipation. Big-time. Imagined us standing at Cabo da Roca, the westernmost point in continental Europe. I thought I was Vasco da Gama, when in reality the only sailing vessel I know is the Staten Island Ferry.

Instead, the three days we were in Sintra, where the Portuguese royal family summered in splendor, and the last two days of the trip back in Lisbon, we got very wet. The rain was accompanied by winds that found us, no matter how we positioned our umbrellas. We kept ducking into palaces covered in Moorish tile and into *pastelarias,* piled high with custard-filled *pastéis de nata,* to dry off and drink espresso. Such hardship. Part of the challenge arose from the lack of clean clothes. Whereas we discovered that food and drink were extremely reasonable—indeed, half the price of restaurants in Great Barrington—you had to be filthy rich to get your clothes washed in Portugal. The hotels and B and Bs we stayed in charged by the piece. So you could spend 8 euros, or $10, getting your pants washed. There was no understanding it.

I rinsed out a few pairs of underwear made of some nylony material that was willing to dry. But socks, forget it. We eventually found a *lavandaria* where there was a woman who charged 2.85 euros per kilo to wash your clothes. But before that, the footwear situation had become quite desperate until we ran into a general store where an Asian woman maintained an inventory that included toothbrushes, scrunchies, frying pans, thumbtacks, and socks, among a great many other things. I thought she might have been from Macau, which turned the purchase of socks into an encounter with the influx of empire, a reminder of Portugal's rapacious past. In the store, we each bought a three-pack of socks for a total of 4 euros. In this lovely, no longer grandiose country the size of Vermont, you are encouraged to buy things, but you are not encouraged to wash things.

A day or two before, I bought a wool hat in Monforte, deep in the countryside. I bought the hat in another store with a grab bag of merchandise, also owned by Asians. People from the East seem to be in this "If you need it, we've got it" business in Portugal, the way, in this country, if you want your toes painted, the pedicurist will be Vietnamese. I wasn't in Portugal long enough to discern what the Angolans and people from Mozambique and Goa were doing for a living. But you can feel the presence of populations from faraway places and witness the history of the past centuries in the street. On our second night we got lost in Lisbon looking for a Brazilian restaurant. There are no street signs, the names of the streets posted directly on the corners of the building . . . sometimes. We climbed and climbed up the very steep limestone cobble, stopping periodically to play charades with people standing on corners. "*A esquerda?*" pointing dramatically to the left. She shakes her head back and forth. "*A direita?*" "*Sim. A direita.*" We turn hopefully to the right, and there it is, the hole-in-the-wall Brazilian restaurant we've been looking for. Only problem is, it's seven o'clock, and the place doesn't open until 7:30, so it's locked. But we knock enthusiastically, and the owner comes to the door and lets us sit at the bar, where her husband mixes up a batch of caipirinhas, Brazilian cocktails made from a concoction of fermented cane alcohol, called *cachaça,* sugar, and lime juice, confirming one of the deep truths about being away from home. A good drink and a pair of dry socks in any language goes a long way.

Coco Loco

MANY years ago in Tobago, an enormous iguana fell out of a coconut palm and landed on top of me. I was looking up to see why several men were shaking the tree with great enthusiasm and determination. What was for them a hunting expedition, a business opportunity, became for me the prototype for all travel worth the price of a plane ticket. Something not listed in the brochure falls into your lap, takes you completely by surprise, and turns your head around.

A relative of the Caribbean iguana seems to enjoy relaxing poolside here in Costa Rica, where I have taken a trial separation from the unforgiving New England winter. The guidebook says this reptile, *garrobo,* two feet long with ashy gray and slate blue scales, is reminiscent of dinosaurs. It is possible that the Fodor's guy spent a lonely childhood in outer-borough movie theaters watching nightmare-inducing double features, but to my knowledge, dinosaurs only live in the lurid imaginations of five-year-old boys.

Still, *garrobo* cuts an impressive figure sauntering in and out of the jungle landscaping and up and down the turquoise and white faux-Spanish pool tiles. Occasionally, for a change of pace, he climbs up a long flight of stairs to an upper deck and leaps into the air, crashing out of the Jurassic period and onto the tile roof of my bungalow. This is a killer just before dawn, when I'm savoring the last frames of tropical dream time, trying to crawl back into the ooze. *Garrobo* goes about his prehistoric business, undaunted by the hotel's intermittent water pressure and Wi-Fi connection, unmoved by the young girls in thongs who ripen in the hot street like mangoes on the vine. He's been around, like me, and merits respect, a seat on the crowded bus commandeered by a fellow passenger shouting *abuela! abuela!* when I climb on board. *Garrobo* is like the aging expats, mostly gay men, who gather on Saturday afternoons at Dos Locos in Quepos to listen to the Pura Vida Social Club. The band is playing a BB King–inflected set that pulses out into the torrid downtown from the open restaurant. Nothing separates the musicians and patrons, late of Houston and Pittsburgh and Atlanta, from the *tico* street life. Mothers and babies, trucks unloading. The expats are ebullient, demonstrative. They are all hugging each other. One seventysomething man says to another, "I heard you went up north. Is everything OK?"

The first few days in Costa Rica, I was preoccupied with parasailing. Every day at the beach, I would watch the silken material balloon up behind the person running those last few steps on land to catch up with the speedboat accelerating at a fantastic rate, until suddenly she was airborne, hanging above the lukewarm ocean. I thought, *Si como no?* Why not? At night, when I tried to sleep, I would be plagued by the existential dilemma, to parasail or not to parasail. Think of the post-vacation bragging rights, especially if I went up in the salmon-tinted sunset while the people on the beach were all sipping Coco Locos. In the end, I didn't do it, and I'm glad. I just couldn't see the iguana in my lap. Only pride and vanity wrinkling my skirt. After all, the real stories, the essential stories, need time to incubate, time to hatch. They aren't the ones you can't wait to tell.

What Slips through Your Fingers

EVERYTHING that matters to me is evanescent. Infancy, daylilies, serenity. Sound, taste, color. I know I'm on to something holy when I try to grab it and it slips through my fingers. Even great art can't corral it. Matisse applies paint to canvas and leaves me something that makes a reference to permanence. But color itself can't be made material, can't be hung on a wall, or worn around my wrist. It's a vibration that enters my consciousness when I allow it in and sometimes grabs me by the neck and demands I pay attention to its fleeting hereness. Look at me, damn it. Look at the way crab-apple blossoms send out beams of raspberry mixed with grape-juice stain. I dare you to snare that shade and deposit it in the bank.

Everything begins with green. Green in spring and summer is so pervasive, so customary in the Northeast that I take it for granted. I would be a different person if I woke up to the cream-caramel-pink of sand. I would be a different person if spirit had chosen a fire engine red as the woodland wallpaper. Unimaginable. I rejoice at the return of green after the white-gray-brown winter, and I want to write devotional prayers and love poems to it. But green is unimpressed. It just is, and then it is not.

Set against the green outside my barn-red house right now is a purplish-rosy palette of magenta centaurea, cranesbill geranium, lipstick weigela, and two different baptisias, one lilac, fading into an aristocratic gray. An arrangement of blush, fuchsia and watermelon-colored Japanese primrose in the back garden is now past its season after sprouting up from seed donated by a friend. How do they do it? How do they grow and send out their own particular flavor of holiness, their own now-you-see-it-now-you-don't wavelength of the forever white light? The finite, the fleeting, the mortal arising out of the infinite.

Life's like that. Color itself, so defiant, so resistant to capture, makes a worthy object for contemplation. I'm aware of turning to it when I need a break from the effort of struggling with myself. Who else, after all, do I know well enough to struggle with, who else puts up such a good fight? I allow my gaze to settle on something in my field of vision, anything at all, a coffee cup. I say, "Look at the blue decoration on the cup." Blue. I make a mental note of it and somehow know that it's only passing through. Like my mother very late in the day of her life, sitting on a bench with me in Berkeley just before nightfall, looking up at the persian blue of the California sky, the first stars flickering.

Again, I am transfixed by babies and small children. The perfection of their fingers, their lack of guile. These are not my children or grandchildren, who all carry complex narratives of my invention. They are just centers of radiating warmth in little buttercup-yellow dresses, monkeying their mothers at the Coop. They are the small children who watch in graced unknowing as the wrinkled veterans ride by in the Stockbridge Memorial Day parade. That's the thing about babies and flowers. They wear their evanescence well.

The Persistence of Nature

WHO are the people who feel what the earth feels? Who are the ones who do not position themselves outside nature, looking on with varying degrees of empathy, but understand instead that they are embedded in nature, that their cells are the cells of dromedaries and daffodils. Without them, the weeping earth might experience an even greater sense of abandonment. But nature is persistent. It doesn't give up easily. So even as skyscrapers rise like Towers of Babel over the teeming streets of coastal cities, thrusting uninhabited penthouses into the clouds; and even as the sea rushes over the streets at ground level and the water we drink is contaminated, nature gives birth to certain people who are indigenous speakers of its original language. These people are here to translate the stories of tigers and typhoons to make them intelligible to the rest of us. They are here to bear witness from inside the integrity of the cosmos, to give testimony to its grief and its yearning to communicate. They travel incognito, like *Lamed Vavniks,* the thirty-six holy people of Jewish spiritual culture said to exist in every generation, who in their essence preserve and transmit sacred teachings without ever identifying themselves. It may be that they don't even know the purpose they are serving. Still, without them, the rest of us would stumble along, messing with the syntax, missing the nuance. Most of us can't grasp the long arc of nature's narrative. We are still learning the vocabulary. We think that the suffering is happening somewhere else out there, that we aren't all breathing the same air. If we are fortunate and watchful, we may stumble upon a teacher who invites us deep into the forest. Meetings between generous teachers who have something to pass along and students who are hungry for learning are not arranged marriages. They arrive like thunderstorms, unexpectedly drenching us in awareness, lifting the veil from our eyes, and illuminating the murky, cluttered world so that we can see its heart.

My grandson is that kind of teacher. Here he is reaching out to caress a snake like an Appalachian serpent handler, familiar and unafraid, but without the religious fervor. Here he is arranging his backyard vegetable garden according to the inclinations of the plants, tomatoes next to basil, as if anticipating our human salad preferences. Standing knee-deep in the creek, with his sun-bleached hair winding its way down his back, he is the kind of boy who says getting bitten by a snapping turtle one day in July was his best birthday present ever. It hurt, of course. But he respects the way of the turtle and rejoices in their meeting. He is the kind of boy who floats down the river in a kayak and stops for a long minute to make eye contact with a motionless deer who stares back at him in some kind of appreciative recognition. Somehow, he has inherited the gestures of the Ojibwa and Dakota, native to his home in Minnesota, and wakes each morning to the commotion of modern urban life, feeling somewhat displaced, unnerved. I imagine that being born into the wrong time, the wrong sensibility, possibly even the wrong species, might be a little like being born into the wrong gender. He might be literally a fish out of water. To cross into the other nonhuman world, he will spend hours with his pole and line at the pond or the creek and wait for one of his fellow creatures to visit. Then he will carefully remove the hook and throw the catfish back where it longs to be. It's their brief time together that sustains him and that gives him the intimacy with animal life that he craves. He is continuous with the natural world, an intermediary between its infinite secrets and the hooks that the rest of us hang onto. Without him, I see the trees, but rarely the forest. To me, his city-born grandmother, he is a necessary link in the chain of being. Just a boy doing a boy's thing, but also an adept, a messenger, and interpreter from the great unclothed world.

Less Time, More Space

I remember exactly where I was fifteen years ago when I first heard a spiritual teacher use the word spacious. I was standing beside an enormous desk in a tiny room, more of a hallway really, talking on the phone to a rabbi in Seattle. I knew immediately that the experience of claustrophobia, of imprisonment, was at the root of all my struggles. Ventilation saved me. Not literally opening the window, but oxygenating the narrow capillaries of doubt and fear so that I might be able to see what's out there.

As a child, I experienced a dash of both agoraphobia and claustrophobia. I was visited by nightmares featuring enormous indoor spaces like the Metropolitan Museum of Art, where there was nowhere to hide. At the same time, it was hard for me to breathe in small places, the filthy bathroom up the crooked stairs to the attic of my father's antique store. The comfort zone of my personal geometry originated in the five-room New York City apartment where we lived, neither large nor small. It took decades to inhale and exhale into the world outside of that apartment, that family.

Even now, I am preoccupied with space. The outer space of nebulae photographed in the infrared and spiral galaxies in the ultraviolet. The inner space where, on the far side of the somewhat arbitrary boundary of my skin, my memories and intuitions lie in wait, as immaterial as the solar wind. In the middle distance, all the rest of it, the space between you and me, the space between my house and the one next door, the space across the Arctic tundra, the Gobi Desert, and, most remarkably, the subatomic space between particles. All that emptiness we can't even see. The great discovery turns out to be that what's out there is mostly nothing. No walls to close in on you. No fences to separate you from your heart's desire.

Time is a tyrant. It swaggers through all this nothingness, staring straight ahead, a bit of a bully. Time makes things happen, whether you like it or not, while space just is. Without time, without decay and mortality, space is the Garden of Eden before the picnic. Growth, awareness, suffering, art are all a function of time. In this science fiction movie we call life, we are called to dance with time in empty space. The universe continues to expand. There is more and more space, but the number of chapters remaining in my particular book of life continues to dwindle. There is less and less time.

One way I manage that is to tango backwards, back through history and, better yet, prehistory, so that time is liberated from the hourglass, so that I can experience its elasticity. Human civilization has been around for a nanosecond, a sliver of space-time, only a little more than 5,000 years. Machu Picchu, Chinese porcelain, Venice, fish tacos. We are all infants in the light of geological time. Scientists tell us the earth was formed some 4.5 billion years ago. I swim in that temporal spaciousness when I go down into the limestone cave in my basement. My house, an 1884 two-horse barn, sits on a limestone shelf. The rock is what remained of the coral after the saltwater receded in western Massachusetts. This part of the world, scenic with haystacks and church steeples, was once under the Atlantic Ocean. It was more like Buccoo Reef in Tobago, where we snorkeled at the turn of the millennium. The fish were chartreuse and aquamarine. The creatures in the basement are gray and brown. The ocean has retreated.

Now, with the clock ticking on my sojourn on the planet, the practice of extending my vision in both exterior and interior space-time has become increasingly healing. I understand when a friend facing surgery goes to the beach to visit the "blue doctor." The ocean is ancient and panoramic. Like a Victorian consumptive, I breathe better in salt air. The distant horizon dissolves the artificial boundaries I have created. Going to the ocean is like breaking out of jail. But I don't need to get in the car to travel. I practice contraction and expansion, an accordion-pleated way of being. Inhale. Exhale. I breathe in and focus on what is directly in front of me. Purple vinca. I breathe out and hear the prehistoric ocean rushing through my house. Both geometries stretch my awareness, opening me to the long view, backward and forward, and the wide-angle shot, this way and that.

Beyond Nostalgia

NOSTALGIA is a cheap street drug. When you first inhale it, you get a fierce rush—Lenny Bruce at the Fillmore East! Dylan at Gerde's Folk City! Then comes the inevitable crash, and you are left weak in the knees. You find yourself in the graying present, digging deep in drawers full of loose photos, some snapshots, some formally posed. An overgrown English garden of images not at all like the manicured files of the digital now. Everything so long ago. You look back through a reverse crystal ball at all the hoopla, sometimes not even believing you were there in that time when both you and the world around you were so raw and unfiltered. Adolescent anguish, art, and sex flying in all directions, rocking and rolling off the wall like so many billiard balls. No time to sleep. No idea that you would some day grow old and no longer be the headline.

Yet here you are, Dustin Hoffman's eightieth birthday come and gone, in a world constipated by plastics, still alive despite your various transgressions. You and the world both. At a recent reunion lunch with a dear old friend, you find yourself asking, as each name from the past is wondrously conjured up, Is she alive? Is he still with us? Remarkably, all the people you ask about have survived. They are out there in Brooklyn and Boston and Berkeley, a whole generation of clocks winding down. All you can think about is the two of you and a third friend, in life an anthropologist, waiting for a bus one night in Sunnyside, Queens. The other guy said something so hysterical that the three of you laughed right up to the borderline of wetting your pants. You actually remember the joke, but you can't repeat it. Not because it's tacky or sophomoric, but because it makes no sense. It's embalmed back there in 1963.

Your friend says that seventysomethings hit the jackpot, growing up in the Howdy Doody fifties and coming of age in the hallucinogenic sixties. It's a kind of demographic exceptionalism that may or may not be true, but is probably not possible to evaluate from the inside. You only know what you know, but you're fairly sure there was more to it than tie-dye. The problem with nostalgia is that it's all about yearning. It wants what it can't have. It wants to stay up until the early hours carousing, even though sleep is now its bestest friend. It draws its oxygen from the maudlin belief that there is such a thing as the good old days, leaving out the inconvenient Freedom Summer murders, the massacre at My Lai. It is vulnerable to commercial exploitation. Don't miss the Woodstock golden-anniversary celebration! Nostalgia wants to be reassured that nothing has really changed, even though your mother and father are no longer here to advise and cajole you. Even though you are now the crone.

To really cash in on the jackpot, you would need to consider its impact on the present, to recognize the cellular imprint of the raucous times you lived through on who you are now. To your simmering genetic stock, your ancestral and family history, you would need to add the peppery spice of those improbable times of your becoming, back then before you knew anything about anything, anything about life. There was no cookbook to explain the process, no freeze-dried ingredients to reconstitute. Everything was made from scratch. Everything was improvisatory. You made it up as you went along, which made you deeply foolish, but also somewhat brave. You accumulated experience and squirreled it away for possible use at a later date, going to college in 1962 barely able to find Vietnam on the map, ending up marching on the Pentagon five years later. You graduated into a vast blankness, having no idea what to do with your life, but hitchhiked into adulthood carrying on your back a fragmented, out-of-focus understanding that life itself was precious, and finding yourself thirty-five years later providing pastoral care at the deathbeds of hospice patients.

You came of age in a time of expansion, of dissolving boundaries, of greater permission; and this permission to wander without a plan, without a map, has made of your life one big seminar, Lenny Bruce and Dylan two of your many teachers. Learning has been the hidden paradigm, the holy book; and this gospel, this Torah, has sustained you and lifted you out of a conventional girlhood. It has carried you through loss and disbelief, and will deliver you wherever it is you're going.

Improv in the Subjunctive

IF I had to do it all over again, or more to the point, if it turns out to be true that you *can* do it all over again, I'd like to come back as an archaeologist. I see myself going out in the egg-frying sun with a child's beach shovel, a canvas bag, and a gin and tonic, wearing a big floppy white hat and digging for the relics of ancient civilizations in Palestine. It will be hard work, but I have a nose for antiquities, 4,000-year-old shopping lists in Ugaritic. I like the jigsaw puzzle part too. Lining up the clay shards to see if I can make out some syntax. Two jugs of camel milk, one sack of wheat, and half a dozen figs for drying.

If I could do it all over again, I'd have a great many children, soft daughters with olive skin and curly hair who would inherit my dance moves. They would have babies and more babies, making me a matriarch in a forest-green muumuu, with a big floppy white hat. We do love eccentricity, we elders. We want to believe that we can still do wild and crazy things, downtown things. In my case, contending with all those years of thinking I had to be just like someone else, and a shifting someone else at that. Then, all of a sudden one morning, after a quick avocado toast, I just wanted people to recognize me for who I really am, my letter in Torah.

During my time off from my job as an archaeologist, I'd like to be a jazz pianist. That would be so cool. It would be where the improv came in, all those notes cascading down out of a D-minor seventh. I would shut my eyes and lose myself like the broken fragments buried in the desert sand. Consider this: No one knows what the ancient music sounded like. Was it country-and-western plaintive? Was it in-your-face hip-hop? *I* would find out, and not through dusty, fusty research, but through streaming it inside my memory. Once I heard it, this pagan hit parade, I would sing the secret tunes to all those daughters and granddaughters. We would turn them into the musical scores of little vaudeville shows that we would perform in the kitchen, the Tigris and Euphrates two-step, juggling plums and pomegranates.

I'm speculating on possible alternative lives or variations on the theme of limitation and regret because my friend Alice died yesterday, and it sets one to thinking. I always imagined that I wanted most of all to be single-minded, in the service of a good cause, of course. Kind of like the notorious RBG, who is, after all, short and Jewish, making her the perfect role model. But it turns out that what I have really yearned for all these years is the capacity to be openhearted, expansive, curious. I see myself, the imaginary matriarch, sitting under a flowering cherry tree with all the children at my feet, reading my favorite stories and poems, *The Owl and the Pussycat, Ferdinand, Many Moons,* maybe even inventing my own stories, like my father, who delighted me by creating a family called the Snodgrasses who would visit me when I couldn't sleep. I would be playful, a person who laughed a lot, gave people birthday gifts of homemade chocolate, and saw the good in others. Are there such people any more, or have they all been swallowed whole by the grief of the world?

You never know, do you? All you can do is witness and hope that the boundaries of the life you've chosen aren't too narrow, too rigid; that you can still have unexpected encounters. Sometimes it's best to improvise, wander into other lives, sift through the sand, dig a little deeper, and play a new old song, as Alice, in her colorful skirts and scarves, was known to do.

On Another Note

NOT-KNOWING is the final frontier. It's the ironic and unexpected last lesson, the learning to un-learn. All I know is that I am, as all of us are, heading inexorably toward a place we *can't* know anything about. Preparing for this inevitability is all about learning to move through the cloud of unknowing, learning to navigate the blur. Like walking in the high mountains through a dense fog, not knowing when you might take another step and discover that there is nothing but air beneath your feet.

And here I am with a lifetime of wanting to catalog the particulars. When I was about eleven, I was convinced that I could make a list of all the people I knew. So I took out a virgin yellow pad and a Bic pen and got down to it, beginning with the members of my extended family. On my father's side, a battalion of fleshy Hungarian Jews all involved in some sort of *handeling*, just a few lucky breaks up from the ragpicker. There they are, buying and selling sporting goods in Astoria, linoleum in Inwood, store fixtures, dinner plates. On my mother's side, a much smaller contingent of white collar Romanian Jews. Uncle Jerry the accountant, Cousin Nat the attorney. I wrote their names on the pad. I considered them all in their blintzy, first-generation glory. From there, I progressed to the teachers and people I went to school with at PS 9 on West End Avenue. Michael and Bobby, now miraculously born again on Facebook. Then the kids in my bunk in the Poconos, all of us lined up to salute the flag in our hideous green shorts and yellow camp T-shirts. Next, the neighbors on Eighty-third Street and the shopkeepers up and down Broadway. Bill the butcher, cow blood and chicken intestines decorating his apron.

This illusion of being able to account for everyone was comforting, in the way that predictability is a comfort in childhood. But then adolescence arrived, and junior high school, with kids from other neighborhoods, new stores on the avenue. I couldn't keep track, just the way, some years later, I lost track of all the people I had had sex with. The system was breaking down. Cataloging had been my way of managing the world, a kind of adaptive OCD. I continued to organize information, putting the books in alphabetical order, the *K* of Kafka goose-stepping into the alpine *M* of Mann's *Magic Mountain,* on the way to the serpentine *S* of Salinger. But I couldn't really get a grip on the expanding universe of information anymore. Not even the books, not to mention the galaxies, the DNA, the periodic table. There is too much out there, and I have always been a collector by nature. I've always wanted to know everything. I thought I was free of consumerism, but really, let's face it, my greed for data entry has always been exactly like wanting to buy every pair of shoes in the store.

But now I am forgetting. I treasure you, friends, but sometimes I can't remember your names. It is an involuntary letting go, a mindfulness that has come unexpectedly from my waning mental faculties. Gone the rapid-fire scat. Now I sing on another note, like a long, slow foghorn exhausting its sound. A day at home, especially on the screen porch in summer, is a day well spent. I like to start by writing in bed in the morning, only getting up to pee and carry the laptop, along with a stray blue and white porcelain cup of very strong black coffee, no saucer, back to bed. I like to stay there until my brain empties out and the coffee's gone. Sometimes I have company, but sometimes I am alone with my distant past and the immediate past, with its earthy smell of sleep. Random snapshots from long ago show up uninvited in my mind. Standing in the street on a Saturday in October with some Nancy or Judy throwing a Spalding against the building. Some images are as washed out as a Turner landscape. Whole decades, my twenties, my early thirties, seem to have rolled into the gutter, but I am not chasing after them the way we chased after the pink rubber ball. I'm letting them go. It's a revelation. I can ponder the upside of memory loss, of slowing down. I can become friends with a mind no longer overpopulated with proper nouns.

Just in Case

It occurs to me that I would do well to be more awake, even joyful and less self-involved, just in case lightning decides to strike or my heart inflates to a dimension that my rib cage can't contain. I don't want to be thinking about how I don't like my hair or obsessing about how I may have said the wrong thing to someone last Wednesday at the moment of passage. I'm told that in some traditions, where you're at when you die impacts your adjustment in the afterlife, your access to the more desirable districts. But this isn't my concern. Truth be told, I'm not really a big fan of the afterlife. This doesn't mean that I belong to the "when you're dead, you're dead" school. That seems at least as outlandish and improbable to me as reconnecting with long-lost relatives in heaven—a country club, I might add, that didn't admit Jews when I was a child.

I'm more interested in liminality, in transitions, forks in the road. I see myself being extruded into consciousness at the time of birth. Labored out of infinity and into the world, the here. Then I imagine a cosmic U-turn at the time of death, leaving the world of thingness and returning to nothingness, where all memory is held for eternity. It would be best if these passages were lubricated, right? Slippery, like sex when you're young, not filled with struggle and defiance. You just kind of want to slide in and out. You can sign up for grace if you have time, if you linger. This is a word that has a bad rap. People don't want to linger. They want to get it over with. I understand that there are times when going slowly is painful. Still, for me, linger is a tender, loving word. Like an after-dinner drink.

But what if you don't? What if you are taken by a thief in the night, whisked away into formlessness?

You'll have no time to pack. In your haste, you'll forget the charger for your phone, your sleeping pills—which would be ironic, since there's not much chance of your waking up. I worry about this because I'm attached to knowing what's going on. That's my problem in a nutshell. I still cling to the belief that I can figure it out if I just try hard enough. I will, in fact, solve for x in the mother of all algebra problems. In my more evolved moments, I recognize that the whole point of mortality is not knowing—when it will happen, how it will happen, what it will be like. But then I regress back into a grown-up version of the child's backseat question "Are we there yet?" No, we're not.

If you really want to stuff your remaining time, whatever it is, with worry, there is no end of opportunities. You will be occupied up to your final breath with concerns big and small. You can worry about rising sea levels or air pressure in your tires. You can worry about what to say to some lowlife who cuts ahead of you on line in the supermarket or whether the North Koreans are going to lose it and take the world down with them. Take your pick. But just in case the lights go out, you might want to maintain a supply of ceremonial candles to illuminate your crossing. They can be Advent candles or Hanukkah candles or candles left over from your last birthday party, as long as they shed some light on this fleeting life.

End of Day

ONLY an occasional silo disturbs the emptiness of the prairie. I have never seen anything so spacious, so uncluttered. It's flatter than a large lake on a calm day and more mysterious. I can't wrap my brain around the meaning of the horizon or what lies beyond it. The weather has turned cold, a late-October shape-of-things-to-come cold. All day, the wintery sun has been high overhead in a cloudless sky. The vista has been bright, stark; each barn, each cow defined. The taste of the air is unfamiliar. Back East, the moisture hangs in a low cloud cover, and the maples have refused to turn red. In New England this fall, it has been gray, wet, and busy with insects.

We came out here to visit our son and his family in the Minneapolis suburbs. On the final day of the four-day visit, we all went out to western Wisconsin to close up the cabin for the season. The cabin is a Day-Glo blue trailer perched on fifteen acres above the Red Cedar River. It is light-years away from my native habitats, from vertical Manhattan, from the dense eastern woodland. A foreign country, another planet. It's where the family retreats from the cares of the world, concentrates its energy on staying warm, blazing a trail through the woods to look for the old dog's burial place, playing Rummikub and Uno around the kitchen table.

In the middle of a day of doing the preparing-for-winter chores, putting up the storm windows, pouring antifreeze into the pipes, my son spots a very large bird sauntering into the shed, a run-down outbuilding crammed with lawn mowers, chain saws and scraps of wood. He goes over to investigate. The bird doesn't recognize him as a benign presence, starts to squawk and flap its considerable wings to scare him away. Isaac jumps back and goes looking for the thirteen-year-old, the family bird whisperer. The boy rushes over and identifies the bird, knows immediately who he is and what language he speaks. He's a male ring-necked pheasant, we learn from the naturalist among us. He's stuck back there behind that pile of wood. The boy ventures farther into the shed, approaches the pheasant like a mother leaning into a crib to attend a crying baby. He knows just how to pick him up and enfold the bird in his arms, holding him tightly but not too tightly, stroking him and speaking softly, even bending over to kiss him. The boy's heart opens to welcome the pheasant while we all gather around the altar in the doorway of the shed. I take pictures, craving tangible evidence of the apparition, the holy moment, an encounter between human and bird. Then the boy opens his arms, and the pheasant, massive and jubilant, flies off into the enormous sky.

A few hours later we are leaving behind the cabin, the shed, the river. On the way, we pass through a small town near Menomonie. An imposing stone building dominates the town. The word bank is etched into the lintel of the building, but there's no bank in there. On Main Street there's a pizza place, a number of taverns, and a chiropractor. Also a pharmacy, a Lutheran church, and a Dollar General. If you're not a local, not much seems to go on in this town. If you are, it's where life happens. We are heading back to Minnesota, the same party of six, but changed, more inside of nature, less an audience watching it unfold. It's dusk, and because we are driving west, the sun sets for hours. What we witness through the car windows is not the splashy electric fuchsia and flamingo of a Maxfield Parrish sunset or a giant tropical fireball disappearing into the Caribbean, tourists downing guaro sours and applauding the divine sleight of hand. What we see from the Chevy is a pastel lilac spreading in all directions over a thin strip of Navajo turquoise at the horizon. It's a Midwestern end of day, modest and reticent, as if the sky itself, uninterrupted, is being mindful of not taking up too much space. The sky is my teacher. I shall not want.

www.ingramcontent.com/pod-product-compliance
Lightning Source LLC
Chambersburg PA
CBHW070303100426
42743CB00011B/2321